Leadership and Ethics—Major Ingredients of the Business Recipe

A Guide to Leadership, Ethics, Teamwork and Motivation in the 21st Century

Published by:
Dr. Maxwell S. Pinto
Copyright (c) 2014 by Dr. Maxwell S. Pinto

****

ISBN 978-0-987-7504-7-1

Maxwell S. Pinto

During the preparation of this book, several books were reviewed and lost due to an unfortunate incident. I thank the publishers and authors of those books and sources that I accessed on the Internet and I apologize for not being able to include their names in the bibliography.

Dedication

This is my fourth book on business management. Like its predecessors, this book is dedicated to my family and friends, who have always encouraged me to write books on the subject of leadership and management in the 21st century. Hopefully, this book will benefit students, lay people, businesspersons and professionals alike.

About the Author

Dr. Maxwell S. Pinto is an established business consultant and author, with an honors degree in Economics from the University of Leeds, England and a PhD in Business Administration from Pacific Southern University, California, USA. He is also a member of the Institute of Chartered Accountants (England and Wales) and a Life Member of the Institute of Professional Managers and Administrators (UK). Dr. Pinto is listed in several reputed international publications as a recognized professional.

Dr. Pinto is fluent in several languages. His international experience includes Business Consulting, Corporate Analysis, Management Information Systems, Training and Development, Valuation and Sale of Business, Raising Venture Capital and Administration. Dr. Pinto believes that sound theory promotes desirable practice and that there is always room for improvement.

Dr. Pinto conducts lectures and seminars, and engages in radio interviews in Business, HR Management, Business Ethics, Business Law, Economics and Accounting for graduates, experienced businessmen and professionals.

This book is a follow up to his highly acclaimed and authoritative manuals on leadership and business management, *The Management Syndrome: How to Deal with It!*, *Leadership: Flirting with Disaster!*, *Management: Tidbits for the New Millennium!*, *Ethical Leadership: Fact or Fiction?*, and *Small Business Survival in the 21st*

Century. Leadership and Ethics: Major Ingredients of the Business Recipe represents another attempt to guide leaders from around the world on. Instead of just focusing on numbers, leaders and managers should understand that people matter: their recruitment, training and motivation within an ethical team environment will make the difference between success and failure in terms of corporate goals. Supervisors and others should not disrespect or de-motivate employees. An ethical approach to business is non-negotiable.

Dr. Pinto has a specific commitment to working with business persons, leaders, managers and other professionals, adopting a bottom-line approach to solving their problems.

Preface

This, my fourth book on leadership and business management, is intended to provide easy, directed reading for those interested in grasping the essentials of Leadership, General Management, Stress and Anger Management, Customer Service, Family Business and Succession Planning, Home-based Business Organizations, Retirement Planning and other areas of business.

The earlier editions of this book were reviewed by businessmen, professionals, students and others. This edition is based on their feedback and reviews.

In the 21st century, life in business and elsewhere is expected to become increasingly volatile and complex. The essentials of leadership and management were covered in my previous books, *The Management Syndrome: How to Deal with It!* and *Leadership: Flirting with Disaster!* My third book, *Management: Tidbits for the New Millennium!* highlighted other areas: Business Ethics, Japanese Management, Trade Unions, Women in the Workforce and Business Continuity Planning, and provided management tidbits to help deal with certain issues in the corporate world. My other books, *Ethical Leadership: Fact or Fiction?* and *Small Business Survival in the 21st Century*, adopted a different approach when dealing with real world business issues.

Acknowledgements

I am indebted to Maurice Pinto; Mark Pinto, M.B.A., Ch.FC.; Krishna Prasad, BSc.; Aley Thomas, M.B.A.; Eusebia Menezes-Pinto, M.A., M.Sc.; Maurice Coutinho, V.P., American Express; Josie Gelacio, B.Ed.; Mari-Jane Sutton; Aaron Pinto, M.Sc.; Esther Pinto, and others whose names I may have overlooked, but to whom I am eternally grateful.

Contents

13

Extended Health Care

Employment Insurance

Canada Pension Plan (CPP)

WSIB – Tax-free Disability Benefits

Accident and Sickness Insurance

Critical Illness (Living Benefit)

Long-term Care Insurance (LTC)

Group Insurance

Premium Rates

Group Disability Insurance

Group Medical Insurance

Insurance Industry Regulations

Rebating

Investments/Financial Instruments

Probate

CHAPTER 1 – 21st Century Leadership

and the Impact of the Internet

The emergence of the Internet has greatly impacted the way we communicate with one another in the business world and elsewhere. In order to operate successfully, one must have suitable computer hardware, software and the right people in place, i.e. those who have been selected on merit (including the ability to operate effectively within a team environment), rather than relationships, friendship or other irrelevant criteria. The Internet may be the "holy grail" of business: it enables people and organizations to be extremely effective.

The Business Environment Involves Human Beings

Information is fundamental to success, but it must be relevant, accurate, timely, clearly understood and imparted in the proper manner, to the right people, or else its usefulness will be diminished. The effective use of relevant, accurate and timely information promotes business and personal success; honest feedback can be very helpful.

Excessive use of the Internet may undermine the value of human contact, i.e. people may communicate via the Internet in circumstances where face to face contact is advisable – such as when they are close to one another! Sometimes, members of the same department of a firm spend a considerable amount of time communicating via e-mail when it would be more productive to have face to face meetings, at least on some occasions.

In business, we sometimes forget that we operate within a human environment, where emotions play a part, because people, unlike robots, have feelings. Therefore, one must understand the nature of the people one has to deal with, what makes them tick and what upsets them. If you approach somebody who is time-conscious, make sure you are punctual and precise, otherwise you will irritate him or her and fail to achieve the desired result. Whereas some people place emphasis on money, others are more conscious of their status, how much they are liked in a firm, how much freedom and power they have, or whether the firm operates in an ethical manner or not. Bear this in mind when dealing with people. Most people have a tendency to exaggerate or lie in order to impress others regarding their actual or potential achievements. This being the case, it is important to read people well in order to gain a strong foothold in business.

Priorities and Establishing Beneficial Relationships

Setting goals and working towards their achievement calls for commitment. People should be aware of their priorities and should act accordingly. One may strive for more power, skills, contacts, money or something else. Be prepared to let things go in order to set and achieve more meaningful goals. Most individuals are unwilling to avoid an important business meeting in order to spend quality time with their families. Instead, they will convince themselves that they are attending the meeting in order to fast-track their career for the benefit of their families!

Be creative: use your imagination when connecting people so that the connected parties benefit, because the parties that benefit from the connection will realize, sooner or later, why they have benefited and should be able to offer you some kind of payback. Focus on the welfare of the connected parties, instead of merely focusing on your own welfare!

The business environment is volatile and involves various different requirements. Re-structuring of companies or downsizing may be necessary in order to deal with competitive pressures. Employees keep switching jobs because job satisfaction is quite uncommon and job security is almost non-existent. In order to avoid this kind of disruption, managers should motivate their employees through respect, teamwork, caring and sharing, training, fair compensation packages, increasing responsibility and challenging assignments, thereby persuading them to participate in solutions to problems and making them feel appreciated for the same. If you treat employees like family and show that you care for them, you will reap rewards in terms of loyalty and performance.

Give credit to those who contribute to your success. Be aware of your weaknesses and work towards eliminating them. In a world of intense competition – both between employees and with outsiders such as other suppliers of the same product or service – one has to be intelligent and rapid in approach or face the consequences of being left behind. "Slow and steady wins the race" is a formula for mediocrity! Although speed is of the essence, quality must never be compromised. The intelligence and speed of an individual may cause others to envy rather than respect him or her, but this should not work to the detriment of the firm in question. Conversations should be precise and the lead time between the awareness of a problem and its solution should be as short as possible.

Always be aware of those who have your best interests at heart and are willing to stand by you in times of need. By the same token, be aware of who your enemies are and try to convert them into friends, by being good to them. Spend your time getting to know people and understanding their strengths and weaknesses, so that you know whom to rely on and in what circumstances. Failure to do this means you could face problems that could stall your career development plans.

Make friends with people connected to your job functions, so that they can ease the burden of work at times. For example, there may be a time when you need the help of someone in the mailroom to send out an urgent piece of mail. It may be preferable to contact him or her directly, instead of depending on your manager to do the needful.

Never compromise on quality or ethics! If the budget cannot stretch to cover certain liberties, communicate this with the person in charge and revise the budget accordingly. *Cutting costs at the expense of the firm's reputation is totally unacceptable!*

Pay attention to the time of day at which you receive calls from people, as this will eliminate the hassle related to telephone tag. Some people like to call in the morning, whereas others may call later in the day. Take note of this and make your phone time more productive.

Customers – An Enigma!

Developing a relationship with clients is based on trust, results and adaptation to their changing needs. Ethics are always important. Therefore, it is unacceptable to build and maintain an income-generating client base by adopting unethical practices!

Customer service must be of the highest quality in a world where mistakes should be minimal. Sometimes it is advisable to apologize to the customer and offer the latter some benefit, so that he or she realizes that you are doing your utmost to satisfy him or her, regardless of the circumstances. The company should also work towards zero tolerance of mistakes, because mistakes can prove costly and irritable to customers, suppliers and others, thus harming the reputation of the business, with adverse implications for the bottom line. That being said, human beings do make mistakes – robots may not!

Be prepared to listen to your customers carefully, so that you can satisfy their (reasonable and) precise needs and improve the bottom line. Sometimes the customer may feel the need for your product, but may be reluctant to use it for fear of displacing an existing product. For example, the customer may have a limited amount of storage space and may be reluctant to replace an existing product which brings in a steady income with an untested product. If a store sells the George Foreman Grill successfully, it may be reluctant to stop selling it in favor of a product that you are offering. Persuade the customer to sell both products and to note which one generates a higher income, within a given time period, while offering an added incentive. Alternatively, it may be necessary to "create" a need in a customer, by (say) selling him a cellular phone or a digital camera, or a cellular phone with a digital camera, when he has never felt the need for either product and is quite satisfied with what he has.

Ideas, Decisions and Implementation

No given individual can claim to know everything relating to his or her role in the organization. Therefore, it is virtuous to admit shortcomings and to work towards eliminating them. Good ideas are useless unless they are implemented in a timely manner. When presenting an idea, make sure that it is well packaged and presented to the decision-maker, so that it receives the attention it deserves and promotes the necessary action. The best ideas need the support of their creator and are therefore difficult to steal. Share your ideas with others and help them. Those who are grateful for this approach will probably return the favor at a more opportune time.

Decision making should be effected on the basis of comprehensive information which is relevant, accurate and timely, analysis of the information in question, experience and intuition, rather than logic alone, based upon a thorough understanding of the facts. It is naïve to assume that people take a rational approach to decision making, because intuition plays a significant role in a world of uncertainty. Decision making should be preceded by careful thought and due consideration. That being said, bad decisions should be reversed, e.g., firing an employee who was hired for the wrong reason and who can no longer perform in line with the required standards.

A certain amount of nervousness helps conscientious people work harder to achieve their goals, be it in business, personal life, sports or any other field. Therefore, if you are not nervous to a certain extent, there is a distinct possibility that there is something wrong. Perhaps you are under-estimating the task at hand, as when Nastase played Borg at Wimbledon in 1976.

Meetings can provide great exposure, if you are well prepared for them and give others a chance to present their views. Do not let such moments pass you by, because they are opportunities to express yourself. Never be afraid to volunteer for a job that would normally require more than your existing skills. Initiative is always admired if you can deliver the goods, as far as the assignment is concerned.

Try to arrange meetings with outsiders on neutral grounds, rather than on their territory, where they have "home court advantage", a distinct psychological boost. You may wish to designate a particular restaurant as a meeting place. Observe people and try to pick up clues as to their nature and operating style. Make a habit of this, and do it continuously. Keeping your eyes and ears open can give you a heads-up, to help maximize the benefits from a given set of circumstances. A little bit of information may go a long way towards helping you. Do not hesitate to pay the bill when you visit a restaurant, thus confirming that you are generous, rather than petty-minded.

Networking usually results in additional business, but do not make it obvious that you are looking for business via a selfish approach. If people get the perception that you are simply interested in what's in it for you, rather than in them, they'll feel manipulated.

Working Style, Fairness and Loyalty

Successful people realize that it is sometimes necessary to step on people's toes. *They concentrate on being effective, rather than merely "nice."* When applying for a job, successful people usually list references that will help inform prospective employers of their character traits e.g. a good heart, as demonstrated by volunteer work for the homeless and the needy.

People should always be aware of their style of working and at what times of the day, week or year they function most effectively. Accordingly, they should structure their meetings and assignments so as to boost their performance. Bosses like people who think and complement them in ability and performance, thus adding value to the business, rather than individuals who agree with them consistently.

We all face crises from time to time. Some of us learn from these crises and improve our performance, whereas others merely complain about how life is treating them.

Managers and others should always be fair in their dealings with others. Treat others as you would have them treat you and you will be blessed in business and personal life, not necessarily in terms of money, but in terms of inner satisfaction that is difficult to quantify in monetary terms. Surround yourself with a circle of true friends.

Individuality, Intelligence and Talent

Every individual is unique; people have different talents. Logic is not the only proof of the existence of intelligence in a person. Accordingly, people should be selected for assignments on the basis of the requirement of specific assignments, their flexibility and their ability to operate as members of the team in question.

Needs and Wants

People's needs and wants change over time. Money is usually an important part of the equation, but other requirements include respect, motivation, a sense of belonging and companionship and a degree of achievement in line with personal goals.

The Employment Contract

The contract of employment should mention what is expected of the employee and the compensation package for his or her commitment. However, it is not possible for the contract to be all-inclusive. There will always be implied terms, based on the expectations of both parties and ethics. Communication between the parties involved, through words and behavior, should supplement the contract and help promote goal congruence and the satisfaction of both parties.

In any relationship, there is an unspoken contract that should not be violated. It is important for both parties to realize their responsibilities, while appreciating the opportunities that exist because of the relationship in question.

Be honest when appraising an employee, whether it is a formal or informal appraisal. Beating around the bush or getting someone else to deliver the message regarding the employee's performance is professionally unacceptable.

An Individual's Work Area

The designated work area of an individual gives you an impression of the person. Common courtesy should be extended to the occupant of a work area, before, during and after a visit to the work area in question. The work area should always be neat and organized. Due attention should be paid to feng shui – a Chinese art of arrangement which promotes harmony and efficiency, while stressing the need to avoid clutter.

The 'Johari Window' concept discusses how we see ourselves, as opposed to how others see us. There are parts of us that neither we nor outsiders are aware of and there are parts that we do not wish to disclose, because we feel the need for privacy.

People form an impression of us based on our behavior, our work area, and the way we dress and communicate, including our body language. People form an impression of a company based on how it deals with employees, customers, suppliers, and the company's premises (in terms of layout, style, decoration, space available for insiders and outsiders and other factors). People should try to work for companies whose style of management and operation fits in with their own style and personalities, thereby causing minimal friction, ceteris paribus.

We should play roles that tie in with our ability, otherwise our performance will suffer, due to miscasting. There are times when we should take (calculated) risks, because, as the saying goes, "nothing ventured, nothing gained." Managers and other employees are given certain powers, which they should use in line with corporate objectives.

Teams, "Knowledge Workers" and Other Matters

Teams should be formed on the basis of the tasks to be performed. Team members should possess skills that complement one another and provide effective solutions through synergy.

Peter Drucker, who was widely recognized as being the foremost management thinker of his time, referred to "knowledge workers" as individuals who possess intelligence, knowledge and the ability to benefit the organization, in return for which they should be appreciated, respected and compensated. They depend on the organization for a source of income and the organization depends on them for their performance, in line with corporate goals. Drucker believed that the world is "becoming knowledge sensitive and that the knowledge worker is part of the evolution of management into a respectable and influential discipline."

Nonaka and Takeuchi, in their book *The Knowledge Creating Company: How Japanese Companies Create the Dynamics of Innovation*, refer to knowledge creation over a period of time, based on the acquisition of knowledge from internal and external sources and its development. They also stress the importance of middle-management as the link between senior managers and workers on the front line.

Charles Handy, a reputed author, successfully predicted the growth of outsourcing, telecommuting, the intellectual capital movement, knowledge workers and virtual project teams. Thomas Stewart, in his book

Intellectual Capital: The New Wealth of Organizations discussed intellectual capital and its components. He claimed that it is comprised of:

(a) Human Capital, which resides in the minds of employees;

(b) Customer Capital, which is the value of the company's ongoing relationships with its customers; and

(c) Structural Capital, which relates to the knowledge retained in the company.

Ethics

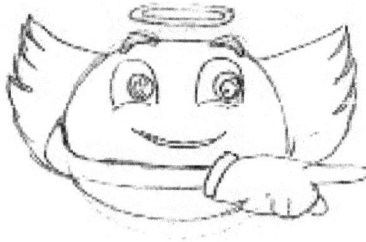

An organization should never compromise its principles. Outdated procedures need to be carefully reviewed and revised. Profitable growth is usually the goal, though not at the expense of principles being compromised, otherwise the organization will be regarded as lacking in substance, and success may be short-lived and eventually wiped out by lawsuits and damages. The pursuit of profitable growth should not adversely affect working conditions or the environment.

Individuals and organizations should understand that unethical practices will not be tolerated under any circumstances whatsoever. While there are some individuals who engage in unethical practices which benefit the organization to which they belong, there are others who engage in unethical practices for personal gains, at the expense of corporate welfare.

Several business enterprises offer seasonal employment opportunities to students who are in need of industrial experience, to complement their education, and make them more marketable on graduation. This provides a win-win situation for the business enterprise and the student in question. In my opinion, the student should be paid a nominal fee as a token of appreciation, assuming that the student displays a keen interest in the job, rather than a tendency to merely go through the motions in an attempt to boost his or her resume'. It is true that there will be a cost associated with training the student. It is also true that the student will add value to the enterprise. Surely the enterprise would not offer the student in question an assignment merely on the basis of love for their fellow man or on religious grounds!

People, Communication, Negotiation and Related Matters

People who have been selected on the basis of merit (including their ability to operate within a team environment), rather than friendship, relationships or any other irrelevant criteria, are the main resource of any organization. Therefore, they should be adequately trained on a continuous basis, allowed to contribute to decision making through participation and brainstorming, thereby reducing the burden on management, and motivated through respect, caring, sharing, challenging assignments, increasing responsibility based on ability, teamwork and compensation, so that they operate in line with *corporate* goals. People should be appreciated for their effort, performance and (classical and emotional) intelligence, which is often as important as street smarts!

Managers should focus on the present, while also planning for the future, based on the need for continuing profitable growth, core competencies and the possible acquisition of new workers, through employment, subcontracts or other means. Managers should be aware of what is happening in the business world and what is likely to happen in the near future and in the medium and long term, based on facts, experience and intuition.

Communication and feedback are always important in any relationship, be it husband and wife, friends, employees and managers, employees and customers, employees and suppliers and even with competitors. In some situations, communication with competitors can help improve business operations, but the importance of ethical operations should always be borne in mind.

Negotiation is fundamental to life and business. The negotiating parties should focus on strengthening the existing relationship through a win-win situation for all involved and continuing the relationship, in the hope of better prospects, through teamwork and co-operation. If people notice that you are interested in their welfare, they will pay attention to your interests and will bond with you, thereby promoting your success.

Although life is complicated, matters can often be simplified by the individuals concerned. In essence, what matters is one's approach to the solution of problems and the realization that some problems cannot be solved completely, e.g., anger and its management. Such problems should be handled satisfactorily.

Leadership, Vision and Approach

Leaders share their vision with their people in an attempt to convert their vision into reality. They must be ethical and must lead by example, while motivating their followers and enabling them to develop into leaders themselves. They

47

must realize that selecting people based on merit, including their ability to operate within a team environment, nurturing them and motivating them will promote profitable growth. Training and development in order to cope with continual change is of paramount importance in these turbulent times of re-structuring and downsizing. People, rather than money alone, spell the difference between success and failure.

Leaders should be optimistic but realistic, otherwise they will be guilty of living in fantasy land. Leaders should welcome positive change. Leaders should command respect through behavior and performance and they should use, rather than abuse, the power that they are entrusted with, so that they can achieve the desired results and enable individual as well as corporate growth. They should lead by example, rather than empty words (see *Management: Flirting with Disaster!*) and share their power in a way that energizes others towards desired performance, while instilling in their subordinates and would-be leaders a hunger for success through positive means and methods. Persuasive communication via the use of appropriate words, tone of voice and body language is often the difference between a good leader and a bad one.

In her book *Never Work for a Jerk!* Patricia King maintains that "forgetful bosses, ignorant bosses and stupid bosses frustrate people and waste time and money. They cause ventures to fail, stockholders to lose their investments and people to lose their jobs. Yet there are thousands of them." As discussed earlier, and without laboring the point, this confirms that employees are often selected and/or promoted on factors unrelated to merit, thus causing chaos and undesirable results. These individuals are normally ill-equipped to make sound decisions or train and guide people adequately, and many of them do not have adequate people skills. We are faced with the problem of the blind leading the blind and leading those who can see!

Talented employees often leave organizations after a short stint because they are not treated with respect and care, on a personal level. This is followed by similar treatment in subsequent jobs, because supervisors and managers are not properly trained for their roles. Research confirms the disappointment of many employees with regard to how they are treated by their superiors. Managers are the main reason why people stay and thrive in a firm or leave with their knowledge, experience and contacts, giving all of these to the competition.

"People leave managers, not companies," claim Marcus Buckingham and Curt Coffman. "So much money has been thrown at the challenge of keeping good people – in the form of better pay, better perks and better training – when, in the end, turnover is mostly a manager issue." *If you have a turnover problem, look first to your managers.*

Are they driving people away?

Bad bosses adversely affect the emotional health and productivity of employees. Criticizing, insulting or degrading employees in the presence of others, being too picky while assuming that you are perfect, and not sharing information as and when required will affect an employee's work and his personal life. The problem must not be allowed to escalate. Some managers are too controlling, too suspicious, too pushy, too critical, and too hard to please. They forget that workers are free agents, rather than fixed assets. When this continues, an employee may quit due to the cumulative effect of seemingly trivial issues. People leave jobs for opportunities or for circumstantial reasons, but many would have stayed, if treated well enough to warrant a continuation of their employment.

The cost of losing a talented employee includes: the cost of finding and training a replacement, the cost of not having someone to do the job in the meantime, the loss of clients and contacts the person had within the industry, the loss of morale of co-workers, the loss of trade secrets this person may now share with others, and the loss of the company's reputation, among other factors. *Every person who leaves a corporation becomes its ambassador, for better or for worse!*

Organizations must have rules and leaders who ensure that the rules are followed. The rules in question should not hinder creativity and profitable growth, within the constraints of good working conditions and care for the environment. Also, respect for individuals throughout the organization, rather than for only the supervisors and managers, is very important, because it gives people a sense of worthiness, wellbeing and of belonging to the family of workers.

CHAPTER 2 – Ethical Leadership: An Oxymoron?

Leadership is about vision, guidance, motivation and desirable results. *Ethical* leadership takes into account morality, principles, integrity, values, caring, sharing, "a green approach" and the importance of participative decision-making.

Abraham Lincoln was the 16th President of the United States. He successfully led the country through the American Civil War, preserving the Union and ending slavery. He said, "When I do good, I feel good; when I do bad, I feel bad. That's my religion." What's yours?

Albert Schweitzer was a theologian, musician, philosopher, and physician who received the Nobel Peace Prize for his philosophy of "Reverence for Life."

Schweitzer's spent much of his life trying to discover a practical ethical philosophy to show to the world. He believed that it was man's (ethical) duty to help (rather than harm) others.

Wystan Hugh Auden is regarded as one of the greatest writers and poets of the 20th century. His work covered morals, love, politics and citizenship. He once said, "We are here on earth to do good for others. What the others are here for, I don't know."

William Lloyd Garrison was a prominent American journalist and social reformer and one of the founders of the American Anti-Slavery Society. He was also a spokesman for the women's suffrage movement. He maintained that the success of any great moral enterprise did not depend upon (mere) numbers!

In an ideal world one could ask *Did you lie/steal/cheat or not?* In the real world, life is not as simple as this. For example, downloading music free of charge from the Internet initially deprives the artists and distributors of the music of income, but could boost the latter's income through referrals that result in sales of the music in question. Therefore, does such downloading constitute stealing or cheating? Personally, as an author, I have no objection to people reading a major part of my books free of charge via the Internet. Accordingly, I have uploaded major parts of my book to enable free downloading through some Internet archives.

One could also consider the case of sports supplements. To what extent is it ethical to consume such supplements? If they are not forbidden legally, does that make them ethically acceptable?

Black, White, and Gray

Right and wrong are black and white, absolute, pure, uncomplicated. Our ethical system and behavior are a function of several factors, including our cultural background, upbringing, education, ego, environment, circumstances and the related stress. Hence, the development of gray areas, i.e. areas where explicit rulings or guidance is not available, is inevitable. Looked at in another way, there are shades of black and shades of white, just like when you go to a paint shop to buy black paint or white paint or when you go to a clothing store to buy a black suit or a white suit. One should strive to maintain ethical standards that are higher than those of other individuals and organizations.

One's image will depend on one's operation within the black, white and/or gray areas. This should always be borne in mind, while continuously improving ethically.

Ego and Language

As adults we have an ego and try to use our communication skills to justify our behavior, while focusing on our own goals. With our innate selfishness, and influences such as friends, family and environment come many gray areas.

Business Ethics

In business, the bottom line is often considered to be *money*, rather than anything else. In other words, many leaders follow the stockholder approach rather than the stakeholder approach (which emphasizes the needs of stockholders *and others*, such as employees, customers, suppliers, the government and the environment).

In a proposed sale, is it the seller's duty to disclose all material facts regarding the product or service in question, should he or she answer each question precisely or merely address the spirit of the question? Is it the buyer's responsibility to find out the pros and cons of what he or she is getting into by conducting due diligence? This is a gray area.

Good Faith

Utmost good faith is very important from an ethical point of view. If the contract does not reflect the spirit of the agreement it should be amended in the light of what was agreed on, even if there is no legal obligation to do so. Focus on a win-win situation for all, so that you may grow profitably.

Right and Wrong – Myth or Reality?

Business decisions often concern complicated situations that are neither totally ethical nor totally unethical. Therefore, it is often difficult to do the right thing, contrary to what many (philosophically-based) case studies will have you believe!

Moral values such as respect, honesty, fairness and responsibility are supposed to dictate our (ethical) behavior, but are often ignored in times of stress and confusion, when one must abide by one's principles. We shall discuss this later on.

Dilemmas and Mazes of Fiction/Non-fiction

1. Business ethics is concerned with dealing with dilemmas that often do not have a clear indication as to what is right or wrong.

2. Leaders frequently have to deal with potential conflicts of interest, wrongful use of resources, mismanagement of contracts, false promises and exaggerated demands on resources, which include personnel.

Business Ethics and Leadership

Business ethics calls for an awareness of social responsibility, including addressing social problems such as poverty, crime, environmental protection, equal rights, public health and improving education. Hence stakeholder theory, the emphasis on public relations, better human resource management and other areas. We are concerned with people, the planet and (how we make) profits!

Alas, many business schools provide some form of training in business ethics, with an emphasis on a philosophical approach, in preference to a practical one. This needs to be rectified in the light of experience in the real world. Taking oaths related to ethical compliance on a regular and frequent basis is a move in the right direction, though not a guarantee of ethical behavior.

Ethics Management in the Workplace

1. *Society.* An improvement in society could lead to better working conditions, shorter working hours, better treatment of women, children and disabled employees, anti-trust laws, regulation of trade unions and business people, government intervention, a healthier environment, etc.

2. *Ethics and turbulence.* The focus on ethics deters people from straying, although it is difficult to alter the basic nature of selfish individuals – think of Bernie Madoff, Conrad Black and Vincent Lacroix.

3. *Ethics, teamwork and the bottom line.* Constant communication and open discussions on ethics fosters a bond between individuals who are keen on being ethical and helps promote teamwork built on good spirit.

4. *Emotional intelligence and ethics.* Research confirms that emotionally intelligent people are often more ethical than others.

5. *Ethics programs, costs, quality and public image.* Ethics management programs promote a reduction in costs related to hiring and firing and treatment of all stakeholders, but leaders must set an example by behaving ethically, instead of merely preaching about ethics.

Ethics programs promote quality products, services, behavior, a diverse workforce and fair treatment. Ethics programs also promote a strong public image, via demonstrations of integrity and honor in preference to an emphasis on money. Compare the way Johnson & Johnson handled the Tylenol crisis and McCain handled the Maple Leaf Foods crisis, with how

(a) Exxon handled the oil spill in Alaska,

(b) BP handled the 2010 Gulf of Mexico Oil Spill, which was the worst in US history,

(c) Toyota handled problems related to their accelerator pedals, electronic systems and other matters, and

(d) Prominent drug companies in the USA handled research and testing of their drugs on children and animals, marketing practices, overcharging and false claims which cost the US government and taxpayers considerable sums of money.

6. *Benefits of ethics management programs.* These benefits include more respect, better teamwork and motivation and an improvement in the bottom line, based on morally sound behavior.

7. *A less stressful life.* More peace of mind and less overall stress normally result from a sound ethics management program.

Ethics Management Programs: An Overview

Business people need practical guidance on how to establish, implement and observe an effective ethics management program, consisting of policies and procedures based on group discussions to guide decisions and behavior. *Employees should be involved in developing an ethics program and in related training and evaluation, thereby encouraging adherence to the code of ethics.*

As human beings, we all make mistakes, but hopefully they are not intentional or malicious; this is better than deliberately ignoring the code of ethics. One should help people recognize and address their mistakes while operating ethically.

Ethics Management – Roles, Responsibilities, and Implementation

1. The CEO should announce the program, champion its cause and lead by example.

2. An ethics committee at board level should develop and implement the ethics management program (EMP). An ethics management committee should be established, to help in implementation of the EMP, training and monitoring and the resolution of ethical dilemmas.

3. An ethics officer should be appointed to monitor progress and resolve ethical problems/dilemmas.

4. An ombudsperson should be held responsible for ensuring strict adherence to ethical procedures, policies and practices.

The Code of Ethics

Consider the following guidelines when developing a code of ethics, from the Six Pillars of Character developed by The Josephson Institute of Ethics, USA:

a) Trustworthiness: honesty, integrity, promise-keeping, loyalty;

b) Respect: autonomy, privacy, dignity, courtesy, tolerance, acceptance;

c) Responsibility: accountability, pursuit of excellence;

d) Caring: compassion, consideration, giving, sharing, kindness, loving;

e) Justice and fairness: procedural fairness, impartiality, consistency, equity, equality, due process;

f) Civic virtue and citizenship: law abiding, community service, and environmental protection.

An organization can be sued for breach of contract if its practices are not in accordance with its policies. Firms must review their policies at least once a year to ensure they are in accordance with laws, regulations and ethical "best practices."

Topics typically addressed by codes of conduct include: the dress code; avoiding drugs; being co-operative, reliable and prompt; maintaining confidentiality; not accepting personal gifts from stakeholders as a result of employment; not discriminating; respecting the rights of other stakeholders; avoiding conflicts of interest; complying with laws; not using the firm's property for personal use; and reporting illegal or questionable activity. Ethics goes far beyond the law.

Ethics Tools: Policies and Procedures

1. Review all personnel policies and procedures with all employees and obtain their feedback on an ongoing basis. Update policies and procedures to ensure desirable conduct, while avoiding ethical dilemmas such as conflicts-of-interest or infringing upon the rights of stakeholders. Ethical behavior should be rewarded while unethical behavior should be punished.

2. To demonstrate corporate social responsibility, firms often institute policies and procedures to recycle waste, donate to local charities, pay employees to participate in community events, pay attention to customer needs promptly and in a fair manner, and so on. Ensure that job descriptions and

performance appraisals are based on fairness and true appreciation.

3. Ensure that all employees are adequately trained in the ethics management program.

4. A grievance policy is required to handle disagreements between employees.

5. An ethics hotline must be in place to allow feedback on an anonymous basis.

Ethical Dilemmas

Ethical dilemmas faced by managers are often complex, and sometimes without any clear-cut guidelines as to what is right and what is wrong. Several factors influence decisions, especially in a workplace with a diverse workforce.

Examples of Ethical Dilemmas

(a) If a customer cannot afford our products or services should we direct him to a suitably priced alternative, which benefits our competitors?

(b) If an employee deserves more money but we cannot afford it, how should we proceed?

(c) If we claim to encourage the hiring of minorities are we justified in disregarding an immigrant on the basis of his very limited command of the English language, do we hire him and suffer, do we hire him on condition that he improves the standard of his English within (say) three months, or do we hire him and pay for him to attend English classes?

(d) One of my employees refuses to be trained by a gay person who seems to be attracted to him. What should I do?

(e) My boss has confided in me about the pending layoff of a fellow-employee and I have promised to keep silent on this subject. I know that this employee is planning on buying new furniture. What should I do?"

(f) My boss plans to give a new opportunity (which I am interested in) to a fellow-employee who is supposed to leave soon. What should I do?

(g) Am I allowed to use the company's computer or telephone system for personal reasons?

How to Solve Ethical Dilemmas

Ideally, ethical dilemmas should be resolved by a group within the organization, e.g., an ethics committee comprised of directors, managers and other members of staff. Methods to address ethical dilemmas include procedures, an ethical checklist and a list of key questions.

The Code of Ethics

The code of ethics cannot possibly be comprehensive enough to cover all situations. Therefore, one's conscience should dictate one's behavior, regardless of the circumstances. *Paying mere lip service to ethics is unacceptable!*

Leaders and managers must realize their vision through people who have been selected on the basis of merit rather than on the basis of any irrelevant criteria such as friendship or relationships. These people should be trained, and motivated through teamwork, caring, sharing, fairness and respect.

1. *Values.* Leaders must establish their own values and the values of the organization and ensure through communication and appropriate training that employees have similar values.

2. *Trust.* Leaders must facilitate trust between stakeholders and outside parties, with a view to promoting effective operations within an ethical framework.

3. *Code of Conduct.* The code of conduct should reflect the ethics and values of the company in question and should be duly communicated to all stakeholders via literature, training sessions and other means *on and off the job.* Ethics and morality go far beyond mere legal compliance. Leaders should communicate with the outside world through words and example, as part of a public relations exercise aimed at boosting the corporate image and goodwill. Feedback should be welcomed to help improve effectiveness within an ethical framework.

4. *Act.* To be effective, the entire firm must demonstrate ethical behavior. All unethical behavior must be reported, investigated and acted

on in a firm but fair manner. A concerted effort should be made to recognize and reward exemplary demonstrations of ethical behavior.

5. *Monitor and Sustain Ethical Behavior.* Ethical leadership is mandatory. The organization must gather feedback through surveys, focus groups, one-on-one interviews and other means to identify stakeholder concerns regarding the presence or absence of an ethical environment. Possible benefits include an increase in goodwill via an improvement in the corporate image, reduced employee and customer turnover, lower legal costs and more desirable results.

Bernie Madoff, a reputed Wall Street Investment Advisor, and one of the founders of the NASDAQ exchange, directed an elaborate fraudulent scheme involving several billion dollars. He had allegedly been running a "Ponzi" scheme – taking in and losing new money of up to several billion dollars, including the life savings of thousands of his clients to pay dividends to existing investors. Mr. Madoff was placed under house arrest, on a $10 million bail!

A federal judge ordered that the mail of Mr. Madoff and his wife be searched by a security firm before leaving his building and an inventory be taken of all valuable portable objects in his apartment every fortnight in order to ensure that he did not attempt to dispose of them. He was later sentenced to 150 years in prison.

Vincent Lacroix was convicted on 200 fraud-related charges to a total value of more than 100 million US dollars and was recently sentenced to 13 years, but may be released within 24 months. This is the largest financial scandal in Canadian history.

There are numerous other significant examples of fraud. The *Forbes Magazine* "Corporate Scandal Sheet" (Patsurius, 2002) listed, among others, names like Enron,

Time-Warner, Bristol-Meyers, Halliburton, K-Mart, Tyco, WorldCom, and Xerox. So whom can you trust?

Enforcing the Code of Ethics

The Sarbanes-Oxley Act (2002), USA was enacted after the Enron scandal, in an attempt to enforce strict reporting requirements and prevent corruption. It is extremely difficult for some individuals to be ethical when tempted by the possibility of huge financial rewards and excitement resulting from corruption.

Non-compliance with the Code of Ethics – The Consequences

Failure to comply with a strict code of ethics can result in loss of reputation, trust, business, and legal consequences. This should always be borne in mind.

Human rights issues are complex. Their importance is often undermined by managers. Violations in this context should be prevented or minimized in order to ensure effectiveness, in an ethical manner. The third report to the UN Human Rights Council, submitted in late 2008, discusses

a) The government's duty to protect human rights;

b) Corporate responsibility to respect human rights; and

c) The need for greater access by victims to effective remedies.

These core principles have been endorsed by major international business and human rights organizations. Many chief executives have firmly committed to the protection of human rights: health care, safe drinking water, decent beverages, safety at work, mutual respect, non-discrimination, and justice on a global basis, while believing that such a commitment will promote goodwill and improve business performance.

Human rights acts are designed to protect employees while taking their feelings into account. There are usually grievance procedures which deal with employees who feel that they have been taken advantage of. If the business organization cannot satisfactorily handle such problems, the offended employee may pursue legal action and compensation through the courts.

Many business enterprises tend to focus on the bottom line rather than on doing the right thing. Many individuals choose to believe that ethics should be confined to the personal side of life, rather than the business side as well. The golden rule to follow is "Do unto others as you would have them do to you." Compliance with the code of ethics may deprive you of financial or other benefits in the short-term but will certainly yield dividends in the medium- and long-terms.

Practical Emphasis and Approach

How do ethics fit in with organizational goals and employee performance? Some organizations specialize in providing business enterprises with guidance in the field of ethics by identifying ethical risks and establishing systems to emphasize higher standards of business conduct.

Employees who observe ethical leaders practicing and encouraging honesty, fairness, respect and trust at work report more positive experiences. Moreover, they are less likely to compromise on ethics or perpetrate misconduct at work, while also deriving greater satisfaction from their job.

Feedback

It is important for executives to welcome feedback from other employees, perhaps on an anonymous basis (in order to avoid acts of revenge against the providers of feedback), and act on the same when developing ethics programs. The approach should itself be ethical in nature!

An Ethics Program: Introduction and Development

Introducing and developing an effective ethics program calls for companywide cooperation through communication, feedback and implementation. Leaders must lead by example rather than speech alone, in their attempt to satisfy stakeholders!

We must clearly define ethics and demonstrate ethical behavior in line with our ethical beliefs. By respecting employees and treating them as part of the corporate family, they will be more inclined to behave in an ethical manner. This will boost the corporate image and attract quality clients, while avoiding scandals and adverse publicity.

In the business world one hears catch-phrases such as "transparency," "core values" and "going green." But there is more to ethics than merely using the foregoing terms. Ethics is defined by the Concise Oxford Dictionary as "the science of morals in human conduct." Training in ethics should be supported by ethical behavior. It is not enough to preach about the importance of ethics while making false promises and unreasonable demands on employees and offering students an "opportunity" to work and gain experience (to help boost their résumés) without paying them even a minimum salary. The law may allow this practice but that does not make it ethically acceptable!

According to many individuals, the latter is a gray area in ethics but according to me it is a blatant attempt to take advantage of such students, who seek employment opportunities during their vacations in order to gain work experience prior to graduation. Similarly, stem-cell research is considered to be a gray area, although many people consider it to be immoral in situations where a "living being" is destroyed to enable "scientific progress."

One should consider what is right and fair and operate accordingly, while making suggestions for improvement in a constructive manner and being positive.

This will contribute to a decent work environment and community. We are living in a world in which corporate scandals have taken their toll in terms of lost trust: BP, Toyota, Enron and Arthur Andersen, Pfizer and other drug companies, not to mention Tiger Woods (regardless of whether or not he can be considered to be a corporation). Jobs are being outsourced to poorer countries in order to take advantage of cheap labor, which includes, in some cases, child labor. Competition is stiff and the emphasis on bottom-line results tempts managers and others to engage in unethical practices in the business environment.

A "green" approach must be genuine, rather than a marketing ploy to attract additional business or a mere exercise in public relations. There are consultants who specialize in helping businesses "go green."

Discrimination on the basis of race, color, religion, sex, national origin, disability, or age still exists in America, despite the Civil Rights Act, 1964. The Act emphasizes the requirement for "zero tolerance" of such discrimination, regardless of whether it is conscious or unconscious.

The opinion of a vast majority of people can often influence a person's thinking regarding ethics and other matters to a greater extent than the influence of the law and a company's code of ethics. The combined opinion of a large number of people can help change the law.

Ethical business or investment is concerned with how much profit is earned and *how* this profit is earned. This approach takes into account social responsibility on a national and international basis and includes due attention to safety issues, the prevention of child labor, honesty, fairness in employment and remuneration practices, environmental concerns, health implications, investment in dangerous products and other matters.

Ethics goes far beyond the law. Some ethical actions can lead to a change in the law, e.g., where there is pressure from many people to ensure equality for all. Ethical actions are not always legal. Interestingly, the UK Consumer Protection Regulations, 2008 considers it illegal to mislead customers. Before the Act in question, such actions were considered perfectly legal, though unethical!

A significant influence on ethical judgment is the flip-side of whatever situation is in question: the effects of the ethical decision. An ethical decision may not be regarded as being sensible if it benefits some people at the expense of more people, i.e. if it is not "for the greater good." This sort of argument is often used to defend unethical actions and policies.

The Basis for Ethical Decision Making – Fairness

In order to be ethical one must be objective, fair and able to see other people's points of view. This is difficult in times of pressure. The following are some guidelines:

1. Be fair – this is more important than boosting your own ego.

2. Ascertain the facts of the situation.

3. Review your previous experience and the experience of others in a similar situation.

4. Appreciate the short-, medium- and long-term consequences of the decision.

5. Be aware of the law related to the matter at hand.

6. Consult people with the required expertise.

7. Ask those who will be affected by the decision to participate in the decision making.

Workplace Bullying – Unethical and Professionally Unacceptable!

Bullying is unethical and professionally unacceptable, because it is a deliberate and repeated display of uncivilized behavior, involving manipulation and an abuse of power (for self-gratification), which gradually destroys a person's mental, emotional and physical well-being, in an attempt to gain an unfair advantage. In schoolyard bullying, the bullies are children, whose behavior is controlled by the leaders, i.e. the school administration. In workplace bullying, however, the bullies are often the leaders themselves, i.e., the managers and supervisors. In such cases, reporting a bully to the HR department, for example, may expose the victim to the risk of even more bullying, slower career advancement, or even termination, on the grounds of being a "troublemaker!"

Workplace bullying includes:

1. Acts of aggression: assaulting a person or destroying their property, verbal abuse, teasing, playing tricks, spreading malicious rumors, half-truths, lies or gossip;

2. Criticizing a person's lifestyle or habits, in an attempt to isolate them socially, weaken their

support mechanism, lower their morale and then bully them;

3. Undermining/impeding a person's work/opinions, setting impossible deadlines, reminding them of their mistakes, taking credit for someone else's job performance;

4. Removing areas of responsibility without cause, or excluding someone from certain projects; threatening job loss, etc., to reduce a person's value to the business enterprise and its top management;

5. Micro-managing an employee, intruding on their privacy by spying on and pestering them, e.g. by insisting that the Internet is a corporate resource and that private usage will adversely affect corporate bandwidth. Results-oriented human beings should have access to their cell phones, legitimate websites on the Internet, and their e-mail accounts during breaks, or (say) 15 minutes of company paid time

during the day, otherwise the cost of de-motivation will exceed the cost of "adverse bandwidth performance" by far!

6. Sexual harassment is a form of bullying: abuse of power and disrespect.

Bullying can be based on race, gender, age, or other attributes. Bullying affects victims and witnesses, in terms of anger, stress and lack of job satisfaction, and results in reduced effectiveness at work and elsewhere, increased sick leave and health care costs, less volunteering by employees, fewer positive remarks about respective employers, all of which thus affect recruiting efforts and other aspects of company wellbeing.

Although employees are usually aware of what constitutes bullying in the workplace, only a small proportion of bullied individuals actually admitted that they had been bullied. According to statistics published by the US-based Workplace Bullying Institute;

• ~35% of US workers report being bullied at work

• ~58% of targets are women

• ~68% of bullying is same-gender harassment

• Whereas male bullies pick on men and women, female bullies tend to pick on women more often than they pick on men!

1. **Question:** What are the typical traits of a workplace bully?

Answer: A show of superiority via body language and tone of voice, constant shuffling of paperwork, snacking, walking around and taking excessive breaks to hide their own inefficiency.

a. Talkers, rather than doers, i.e. those who can't "walk the talk"

b. Nit-picking, i.e. "majoring in minors" to destroy the self-confidence and morale of the victim and take advantage.

c.   Developing special relationships with key personnel to diffuse opposition to bullying tactics.

2.   **Question:** Whom do bullies target?

Answer: Targets include various professionals and non-professionals, on an individual or group basis, if they are not expected to mount any serious opposition. Bullying is more highly prevalent in blue-collar, male-dominated jobs, where the tendency to report bullying incidents is relatively low, for fear of being branded a coward, i.e., for fear of one's masculinity being "put on trial," so to speak. (The same reasoning prevents some men from reporting the domestic abuse that they are subjected to.)

3.   **Question:** Why do bullies get away with bullying?

Answer: Bullies get away with bullying because there are few workplace policies and laws to protect the targets, victims and witnesses of bullying, except in the case of sexual harassment (which is also a form of bullying: abuse of power and disrespect). Moreover, leaders may not be inclined to discourage results-oriented bullies, despite considerable talk about the importance of "business ethics"!

4.   **Question:** What can employees do about bullying?

Answer: Employees can collectively diffuse the situation by identifying bullies, isolating them, exposing them, standing up to them, reporting them to the HR department or to their trade union (if relevant), or even enlisting the support of another bully to confront and neutralize this type of behavior. Training sessions can help, when combined with a confidential reporting structure, although it is difficult to alter the basic nature of certain individuals, who may need counselling.

Several years ago, when I was working as a business consultant, a target of bullying finally punched the bully in his nose, after several warnings from the target to the bully. The resulting medical bill was handled by the employer, in order to avoid adverse publicity and a costly lawsuit.

A less extreme approach would call for an employee who suffers any mental, emotional or physical injury as a result of workplace bullying to sue the company in question and the abusive employee as joint respondents in the claim. If the law does not persuade employers to deal with bullying, economic reality will!

5.   **Question:** How can a candidate for a job identify a bully at a job interview?

Answer: The candidate can review the layout and content of the interviewer's office: chair, desk, walls, etc. and note his or her manners and tone of voice (does he or she make eye contact or turn away when the interviewee makes eye contact?), his or her clothes, and body language. Also, did the interviewer deliberately leave the door open, thereby allowing others to disturb both parties, or did he cut the interview short and cheat the candidate of a job opportunity, perhaps because the latter is capable of displacing the interviewer? If the candidate is allowed to walk around and meet other employees, he or she may be able to identify bullies, based on the above-mentioned criteria.

Many years ago, I was interviewed by the finance director of a company, who introduced me to the president for my second interview. The president, a tall, slim, balding man in his late fifties, sat in a dimly lit room, on an expensive leather chair, probably imagining himself in *The Godfather*, and asked me about my areas of specialization, apart from accounting. I informed him that I had just written a book on business and was looking for a publisher. His response: "What? What kind of book is this, and who would benefit from reading it? Many books on business are not even worth reading!"

I replied, "This book is for those who have spent 25 years sitting in the same chair and who keep looking at their receding hairline in the mirror, and remarking 'I have 25 years of experience'." This made him really angry. A few minutes later he calmed down and I was offered the job as the asst. finance director. (By the way, I refused the offer, because I would be uncomfortable in an unethical environment.)

6.   **Question:** What questions can candidates ask and what clues should they be looking for at a job interview?

    Answer: Candidates should review the company's website, which is basically aimed at promoting the company, to find out about its products, services, the board of directors and managers, to note if women have (almost) equal representation in both areas, and to ask questions where matters are unclear. I once worked for an organization whose board of directors consisted of several men and one inefficient woman, because the "old boys club" wanted to confirm that they believed in "equal opportunities for women" – what a joke! Candidates should ask the interviewer about the corporate culture: is it friendly and caring or not? Make eye contact, while being aware of the tone of voice and body language, in order to determine whether, and to what extent, the truth is being told. Try to ascertain the job responsibilities and hiring policy of the institution: preference for hiring from within or not? Is there an effective HR department?

In the US, bullying is recognized as being detrimental to occupational health, but there is little political or corporate interest in stopping it. Discrimination laws cover race, sex, religion, age, disability, sexual orientation, and harassment, workplace safety, and union-protection laws enable employees to sue on the basis of "a hostile environment."

In Canada, provinces such as Ontario (Bill 168: the workplace harassment and violence legislation), Quebec and Saskatchewan have introduced legislation related to health and occupational safety, which includes bullying in the workplace.

In the UK, bullying is addressed by laws related to harassment, and contractual law (including the law of employment contracts) based on good faith, trust and confidence between the contracting parties, which allows the employee to breach the employment contract on the grounds of constructive dismissal and seek damages (in bullying situations). Case law:

a)   Majrowski v Guy's & St Thomas' NHS Trust [47] wherein an employer was held liable for one employee's harassment of another, and

b)   Green v DB Group Services (UK) Ltd [48], wherein a bullied worker was awarded > £800,000 in damages. Where a person is bullied on grounds of sex, race or disability, anti-discrimination laws apply.

In Ireland, The Safety, Health and Welfare Act 2005 requires companies and employees to prevent workplace bullying or face serious consequences related thereto.

In Spain, bullying is considered within the category of labor harassment.

In Sweden, The Ordinance of the Swedish National Board of Occupational Safety and Health exerts pressure on employers and employees, to prevent victimization at work.

In Australia, workplace bullying is generally tied in with laws related to workplace harassment and safety (with each state having its own laws).

Conclusion

There are several benefits to compliance with ethical standards, including increased loyalty among customers, higher quality employees and lower employee turnover (due to greater job satisfaction and lower stress), a greater number of investors, improved image and increased goodwill based on the public's knowledge of the company and its adherence to ethical standards. The UK Institute of Business Ethics suggests a simple test for ethical decision-making in business. This test involves asking oneself the following questions and being able to answer "yes" to each of them:

1. Transparency: Am I willing to inform the concerned parties about my decision?

2. Effect: Have I tried to minimize the harmful effects of my decision?

3. Fairness: Would those affected by my decision consider it fair?

CHAPTER 3 – Anger Management: The Road to Salvation?

Anger is a normal human emotion that must be controlled! Failure to control anger can lead to problems that could affect the overall quality of one's life.

The Nature of Anger

Anger is "an emotional state that varies in intensity from mild irritation to intense fury and rage," according to Charles Spielberger, PhD, a psychologist who specializes in the study of anger. It is accompanied by physiological and biological changes: your heart rate and blood pressure go up, as do the levels of your energy hormones, adrenaline and nor-adrenaline. You could be angry at a person, such as a co-worker, or an event, such as a traffic jam or a canceled flight, or on recalling traumatic or enraging events. One could argue that a certain amount of anger is necessary for survival. Anger can be dealt with by expressing, suppressing, or calming, as outlined below.

(a) Expressing your feelings in an assertive manner (i.e. being respectful of yourself and others), rather than being aggressive (i.e. pushy or demanding), is preferable when expressing anger. Be precise about your needs and how they can be satisfied, without hurting others.

(b) Suppressing your feelings and converting or re-directing them by focusing on being positive and constructive, while bearing in mind that unexpressed anger can cause high blood pressure, depression, vengefulness, cynicism or hostility. People who are constantly criticizing others and being cynical may suffer from unsuccessful relationships, and counseling may be advisable in such cases.

(c)   Calming down, i.e. controlling your outward behavior and your internal responses and taking steps to lower your heart rate.

As Dr. Spielberger notes, "when none of these three techniques … work, someone will get hurt."

Anger Management, Emotions and Arousal

Anger management is aimed at reducing the emotions and physiological arousal caused by anger. Some people get angry more easily and/or intensely than others and may become destructive or withdraw socially, sulk or become irritable when faced with an unjust situation. The cause of anger may be genetic, physiological or socio-cultural. Some children are irritable from an early age. Many of us believe that it's alright to express anxiety, depression, or other emotions, but not anger. As a result, we may not learn how to handle anger constructively. Typically, people who are easily angered come from families that are ineffective at emotional communication.

Expressing Anger

Expressing anger may actually aggravate an existing situation. Try focusing on the root cause of anger and work towards eliminating it.

Dealing with Anger

Relaxation

Deep breathing, relaxing imagery, yoga and other forms of meditation can help calm a person down, as can additional leisure time, entertainment, sightseeing and holidays.

Cognitive Restructuring

Angry people often overreact and hence aggravate a given situation by stressing other individuals out and alienating them. People who are easily angered tend to be disappointed, frustrated and hurt when the going gets tough. In extreme cases, instead of focusing on the solution, you may need to handle the problem or its cause, pending "divine intervention."

Better Communication

Listen carefully and ascertain the cause(s) of anger, e.g., you like more freedom and personal space, but your partner wants more closeness. If he or she starts complaining, do not retaliate by criticizing your partner, otherwise the latter may feel neglected or unloved.

Humor and its Impact

Humor can defuse rage but should not offend anyone. When you get angry and refer to people in a strange manner, try to imagine what you are saying. If you think of a co-worker as a bag full of garbage, picture the latter sitting at his or her desk. When you feel that things ought to go your way, picture yourself as the king of the whole wide world: an individual to whom every other individual is always answerable, regardless of the circumstances! Then you will (probably) realize that you are being unreasonable.

Changing Your Environment, Lifestyle, Diet and the Need for Adequate Sleep

Immediate surroundings, problems, lifestyle, a low level of intimacy, responsibilities, the quest for perfection and your current diet can cause anger. Always ensure that you have adequate sleep and personal time and space scheduled for times of the day that are particularly stressful. For example, when you come home from work, you may wish to be left alone for several minutes, barring emergencies. This would make you more effective in life.

Controlling Your Anger: Some More Tips

Timing: If you are normally tired at night, try discussing important matters at other times.

Avoidance: If any room in your house is messy, shut the door instead of getting upset.

Finding alternatives: If your daily commute through traffic leaves you in a state of rage, map out a route that is less congested or more scenic or use public transportation.

Being assertive: Angry people need to be assertive, rather than aggressive. You cannot eliminate anger, frustration, pain, loss, and the unpredictable actions of others, but you can change the way you let such events affect you, thus increasing your happiness. You can be polite and in control of your emotions, instead of going overboard.

Ethics, Legal Implications, Public Image and Other Matters

Demonstrations of anger can have legal implications, as in the cases of Naomi Campbell and Russell Crowe. The former, a renowned model and notorious character, is well-known for her temper tantrums, outbursts of anger and shenanigans. Her way of dealing with this problem is by looking at the gloves she wore when working as a New

York City sanitation worker, as part of her punishment for assaulting her former maid, Ana Scolavino.

Russell Crowe, a Hollywood bad boy, was arrested in New York in 2005 on charges of assault and possession of a weapon for (allegedly) throwing a telephone that struck an employee of a hotel in the face. Crowe confessed that he "was upset because he couldn't get a call out to (his wife in) Australia," but subsequently claimed that jet lag, his disappointment over *Cinderella Man* and being separated from his family also contributed to his actions, thereby failing to accept full responsibility for the incident. Later on, when interviewed by David Letterman, he publicly apologized to the hotel employee and paid him a six figure settlement, possibly to avoid a civil lawsuit.

At one of his rock concert performances, Crowe threw in a humorous twist by displaying a golden replica of the telephone in question. Also, while hosting the Australian Film Industry Awards, Crowe showed the audience an old-fashioned telephone and added, "If there are any problems and you do get up here and go on too long, then (say) 'hello' to my little friend."

While performing in a play in Australia Crowe head-butted a fellow actor for screaming at him and calling him names. He explained that his colleagues tried to restrain him by holding his arms, and that his head was therefore "all I had left to hit him with and he f------ deserved it." Crowe believes that anger is a prerequisite for survival and that "... holding and suppressing (anger) is ... bull----."

In 1999, two individuals were accused of blackmailing Crowe, on the basis of a security video showing the actor fighting with a man and arguing with a woman outside a nightclub in Coffs Harbor, Australia. They were subsequently freed on the grounds of insufficient evidence.

Conclusion

The world seems to abound with anger. Problems associated with defiant children and domestic violence are at critical levels worldwide. Some minors are being excluded from schools because of displays of anger and violence towards teachers, fellow students and school property. Corporate performance is being undermined by stress and violence in the workplace. These issues must be addressed in a timely manner otherwise there will be dire consequences!

CHAPTER 4 – The Customer: The King of All He Surveys or Merely an Enigma?

The success of a business, which is often gauged by profitable growth, depends on its leadership, the management of the business enterprise and the satisfaction of all its stakeholders: owners, directors, managers, other employees, customers, suppliers, the community, the government and related parties. In this chapter we shall confine ourselves to discussing the significance of customers. A satisfied customer is like a tree that bears good fruit for the business. Therefore, organizations must work towards satisfying customers (though not at the risk of harming other stakeholders) and building trust. Where customers provide feedback, they act as independent consultants offering advice free-of-charge.

The Customer – Is He (or She) Always Right?

Customers are the lifeblood of a business enterprise; their satisfaction is a major objective, in most circumstances. Sometimes, it helps to ask the customer, "What can I do to make you feel better?" In rare situations, where it seems impossible to satisfy a customer, one is advised to throw in the towel and move on, in a very tactful manner, because the good of employees and other stakeholders should not be sacrificed for the sake of the customer! The old saying, "The customer is always right," is in my opinion not always valid, because leaders must take care of all stakeholders, rather than just customers alone!

On our bad days, we are capable of behaving inappropriately. As human beings we have our limitations and we sometimes regret how we behaved on certain occasions. Some of us get a chance to apologize and patch up our relationships, while others do not. Some of us suffer from too much stress and have an anger management problem, which calls for counseling. The foregoing should be borne in mind when dealing with difficult customers.

Disappointed customers are those whose expectations have not been met. Listen carefully to the customer's words and observe tone of voice and body language in order to acquire a thorough understanding of the problem. Try to solve the problem during your interaction with the customer: do not wait until you lose the customer (and related referrals) to figure out what went wrong!

Sometimes a customer may complain about a product or service and may wish to cancel the sale. Listen carefully to the reason(s) for the customer's disappointment, summarize (your understanding of) the problem and get the customer's confirmation of your interpretation, thereby showing the customer that you care about them. This builds trust between you and the customer. Before offering a win-win solution, encourage the customer to propose a solution, while ensuring that you stay calm and focused on the corporate objective.

Never mislead a customer regarding a product, service, warranty, corporate policy or any other matter. An unethical approach shows lack of respect and will probably cost you in the short-, medium- and long-terms!

Ensure that your sales force is well trained, polite, friendly, honest, caring, curious to find out what the customer wants and willing to probe sufficiently to satisfy him or her. Salespeople should adopt a positive approach that focuses on a win-win solution. In cases where the salesperson cannot satisfy the customer's wants, the salesperson should suggest suitable alternatives, based on probing.

Always thank the customer, regardless of whether or not you make a sale or solve his or her problem. If you have wronged the customer, apologize instead of "bluffing your way" and be sure to provide speedy and fair solutions that reduce his or her stress level.

Most companies aim to achieve profitable growth. Profitable growth flows from a satisfied and growing customer (and stakeholder) base, through referrals and repeat business, coupled with creative management, a motivated work force and innovation. Profitable growth should never be taken for granted. There was a time when people would rush to movie theatres, but in the last decade or so, many people have held back, preferring to wait until the movie is shown (a few months later) on a pay-per-view channel, at a fraction of the cost of a cinema ticket. Others prefer to buy a DVD copy of the movie, whether it's the original copy or (as is sadly common now) a pirated version, which is often available within two weeks of the release of the film in question. The movie can then be watched in the comfort of one's own home, without the need to drive, park and stand in line for a ticket and without the stress related to wondering whether one will be seated comfortably, with a clear view of the screen and without undue disturbance. As a result of this change in attitude, movie theatre owners have lost a considerable amount of business and some have been forced to close down. Movie theatre owners took profitable growth for granted and failed to envision such a dramatic change in the attitude of moviegoers!

In 2003, Fred Reichheld published an article in the *Harvard Business Review* that demonstrated a significant correlation between customer referrals and corporate growth. Together with Satmetrix, an established company, Reichheld used this knowledge to establish the Net Promoter™ score, which refers to the number of promoters minus the number of detractors within a customer base. Promoters are happy customers who refer your products to others, while detractors are dissatisfied customers who are neutral or on the verge of defecting. Tracking and monitoring this crucial metric, according to Reichheld, is the best way to achieve high revenue growth and outperform competitors. One must develop more promoters than detractors and motivate all employees to focus on customer satisfaction.

There is often a lag between the first negative experience with a customer and its impact on the overall relationship. During that lag, customer service personnel can prevent any further damage, via remedial action. Developing customer referrals through promoters is the most effective way of growing profitably.

Successful Customer Experience Management (CEM) programs result from multi-year commitments from the CEO to the lowest paid employee and sub-contractor of the company, on a regular and frequent basis, with adequate support from the sales department. The costs and benefits of CEM should be compared. The customer experience data received must be relevant and actionable and the CEM program must be consistent with key corporate metrics and incentives; for example, the bonus plan needs to be in sync with CEM program goals.

Sharing of Information with Employees

An effective CEM program calls for the sharing of the customer experience data among all related employees, as well as the best practices that arise during the life of the program, once these practices have been identified. CEM calls for customer interaction, memory-jogging notes and due action and is extremely effective in steering the company towards profitable growth, if implemented with care and passion, accompanied by due motivation. Mere statistics do not confirm the existence of an effective CEM program!

The CEM program must ensure that the right people always have access to the right data, in a timely manner. Constraints include the quality of the sample of customers chosen (and opting) for feedback and action and

115

their willingness to reply in a timely manner. Employees should then respond promptly and effectively, otherwise they will lose customers and their referrals.

Customers should envision their suppliers as a holistic organization that consists of several touch-points, rather than a series of unrelated departments. Customer behavior is influenced by customer experience with suppliers. Favorable experiences lead to high customer retention, referrals and profitable growth.

The Internet and immediate customer satisfaction surveys enable the receipt of customer feedback within a short period of time. The financial impact of good and bad customer experiences can thus be established. The costs of pleasing customers can be compared with the benefits related thereto.

Advertising your commitment to customer satisfaction can be a great way to attract new customers, if your actions follow suit. In short, "practice what you preach" in an ethical manner. The key to success is having customer experience data and an actionable plan. Companies must blend new capabilities with the old standards in the following ways:

1. Understand and Appreciate the Data: Effect changes in business policies and procedures in line with data collected from customers.

2. Evaluate Customer Needs: Pick areas that need improvement and act upon them.

3. Redesign the Process: You may have to redesign the processes / steps related to the customer experience. Liaise with your customers, product managers and IT department to ensure a thorough understanding of the customer experience. Define success and ROI metrics during the re-design process to ensure that subsequent measurement is accurate.

4. Deliver a New Experience: Initiate a pilot program to be completed in less than three months, and proceed carefully. Demonstrate success in a timely manner, in line with success metrics, and publicize the results on completion. Provide feedback and financial outcome data to senior management to ensure smooth resource allocation and positive customer experiences.

5. Measure: Update the customer file as you gather and act on customer feedback. Study revenue patterns and establish whether there is an improvement or deterioration in the bottom line. In other words, identify whether your methods and actions were justified. Customer loyalty is related to your products and services, including how you deal with customers before, during and after selling to them. Consistent excellence in customer service is of paramount importance!

Customer Complaints and Feedback

Customer complaints constitute feedback that can be converted into opportunities. The eight magic words to diffuse a dissatisfied customer are: "What can we do to make this right?" Listening to the customer carefully helps solve the problem quickly and inexpensively. Do not assume that technology alone will solve the problem!

Educate Your Customers

Explain the benefits and value of the company's products and services in precise terms. Ensure that customers can provide feedback regarding products, services, customer service and related matters, without undue difficulty, whether via the website, the telephone system, newsletter or any other channel of communication. Follow up for feedback after a sale and find out if they have any suggestions for improvement. Ensure that staff are duly trained and up to date in their knowledge and skills on an ongoing basis.

Customers often find it difficult to evaluate intangibles, such as a visit to an accountant, or to ensure that the same standard of service will be provided or subsequently exceeded. There are some grey areas related to customer loyalty to service organizations. Customer satisfaction is always important, as are inter-personal relationships and the costs of switching suppliers.

Many scholars of customer loyalty believe that suppliers of services, rather than tangible goods, have greater scope for building customer loyalty, largely because of the personal element. Some customers will never consider anyone other than their existing supplier(s). Some customers will blacklist certain suppliers.

Customer satisfaction does not always lead to customer loyalty, for reasons which are somewhat unclear. Researchers continue to be puzzled as to which factor(s) guarantee(s) customer loyalty. Many customers are almost always on the lookout for cheaper products, while assuming that quality does not differ between similar products or services. Customers may decide not to switch suppliers because of the time, effort and related costs involved in ending existing relationships and building new ones (switching costs). Research has confirmed that interpersonal relationships are particularly important in the development of customer loyalty towards service providers. In the retail world, where giant stores and franchises are becoming the norm, small business owners can succeed by engaging in more formalized planning, such as sales promotions, and exceeding customer expectations related to quality and service, on a companywide basis.

Summary

Your CEM program should focus on the customer sincerely and dividends will flow. Mere talk about customer satisfaction is not enough to promote profitable growth: appropriate actions should confirm the organization's commitment to customers (and other stakeholders).

CHAPTER 5 – Family Business and Succession Planning

Introduction

The majority of businesses worldwide are family-controlled and -managed, yet leadership and management books and related courses discount the significance of the "family" component in most businesses. Professional advisers to family-owned and -operated businesses focus on the technical component of succession (e.g. tax minimization, estate freezes, family trusts, buy-sell agreements and wealth management), with little attention being paid to the "family" component: family communication, family expectations, family values, family competencies, family dynamics and related matters.

Research confirms that approximately 70% of family businesses will not survive into the 2nd generation and 90% will not make it to the 3rd generation, largely because of family-based rather than business-based issues. Succession issues involve transitioning the management and ownership of the business to the next generation of family members through the application of family business best practices. This should be handled with the current owners and the active family members, while informing the broader family of the outcomes. The trusted advisers should facilitate the process through appropriate advice and monitoring.

The Family Component

The "Three Circle Model" outlined below illustrates the impact of the family component on the management and ownership of family businesses. The "ownership" circle represents the impact of the owners on the family and on the management of the business. The "management" circle represents the impact of management on the family and on the ownership. The "family" circle represents the impact of the family on the management and on ownership. The first two circles are common to all businesses, but the family circle is unique to family businesses.

The conventional Three Circle Model, shows the family circle as having a huge impact on the management and ownership of the business, with the latter functions being normally vested in the family. Therefore, the ability of family businesses to outperform their non-family counterparts and successfully transfer the business to the next generations is dependent on their ability to manage the family component of the business.

Family businesses can provide numerous benefits to family members, non-family employees, and their communities. Family members in business tend to demonstrate a greater sense of passion, loyalty and commitment to each other and to the business. Family businesses favor passing ownership to the next generation of family members, thus providing further motivation to perform beyond expectations. Problems include the possibility of conflicting goals, values, personalities, expectations, work ethics, choice of employees, compensation packages, lack of formal planning and related matters.

The challenges of family business include:

1. Resolving conflicts among family members in the business;

2. Formulating a succession plan;

3. Developing a strategic business plan;

4. Developing a retirement and estate plan.

Family Business Best Practices

Family-owned and -operated businesses need customized solutions for effective management of the family component based on existing best family business practices. Identifying what needs to be done, when, by whom, and how can be a daunting task for the family business. Family business practitioners understand all three circles – ownership, management, and family – and how they interrelate. They can help family businesses manage the all-important family component during the succession process.

Succession Processes and Activities

The family business succession plan comprises the management succession and the ownership succession processes, each with its own set of activities. The management succession process should precede the ownership succession process, and the latter must support the former. There are a number of activities to integrate family members into the management and ownership succession processes and to make them feel comfortable regarding their future.

Family business meetings (FBMs) for the active family members, family council meetings (FCMs) for the broader family, and family business rules help guide the succession process, the effective management of the family component, the grooming of successors, and the integration of the active family members into key management activities. The ownership succession process comprises the same channels of communication (FBMs, FCMs, and the family rules) as in the management succession process, but different types of succession issues are discussed.

Desired Outcomes

The current owners must be comfortable with the management and ownership succession plans, and with the necessary assurances regarding skills, commitment and values, because of their investment in the business. The next generation of owners must be comfortable with the proposed roles and responsibilities of the management succession team, the compensation philosophy, the

128

distribution of wealth, and the funding of the ownership transition, otherwise they may delay implementation of the succession plan.

The succession strategies should be approved by the current owners, and provide both parties with the necessary comfort levels to implement them. In order to manage the family component of the management succession process, the business should consider the following:

1. Who is to lead the management succession process;

2. Communication through FBMs (active family members only), FCMs (the broader family members), and family business rules (guidelines/policies/rules to guide the succession processes);

3. Family members as managers: training, compensation and performance reviews;

4. The role of family members in business planning; and

5. The role of family business practitioners.

Management must state where the business is headed and how it will get there. Everyone must understand the company's goals and strive for their achievement, bearing in mind the family component.

Communicate! Communicate! Communicate!

Many family businesses fail because of lack of effective communication among family members. Family business meetings and family council meetings enable sound communication.

Family Business Meetings (FBMs)versus Family Council Meetings (FCMs)

FBMs involve *only* family members who are *active* in the day-to-day running of the business. FCMs involve **all** family members who have a stake in the business. The same topics may surface at both types of meetings, but the players are different, the setting is different, the process is different, and the desired outcomes are different. If the family can hold effective family business meetings, they should move into a family council setting.

FBMs should address the family component and its bearing on the management and ownership succession, without replacing regular business or board meetings. All active family members need to know who will make specific decisions and how, in order to clarify roles. Other family members or non-family members (i.e. employees and advisers) *can* be invited to these meetings, if beneficial to the outcome.

A comfortable setting and initial agenda items that are non-threatening, non-confrontational, and not overly sensitive will give the meetings a fair chance to prove their value. It may take several meetings before participants become comfortable with the format, the agenda items, and each other. It is extremely important to invest time and energy in getting this step right: a poor start should not be allowed to derail the family business meetings. Regroup, hire a facilitator, and then try again.

Personalities

Some personalities are more aggressive, some more analytical, others more focused on interpersonal relations. Some are risk takers: others are risk averse. Some personalities may clash and cause stressful disruptions within the business. Family members need to make a concerted effort to handle this problem.

Setting up the Family Business Meetings (FBMs)

The owners should assign an active family member to coordinate the time and place of meeting, frequency, rules, issues to be discussed, recording of minutes and other matters. It is also necessary to assign someone to chair the FBMs, and it is well worth considering the benefits of using an outside family business practitioner to facilitate these meetings, especially the first few. The role of the FBMs, the management meetings and shareholder/owner meetings is to make day-to-day business decisions and decisions on succession issues, as well as to develop principles, policies, or rules to guide succession. These latter are referred to as the family business code of conduct, family creed, family charter, or family business rules, to help guide the active family members and prevent or solve problems and reduce conflict. These rules are generally divided into three categories: general, management succession, and ownership succession.

Developing your family business rules with the active family members and reviewing them with the broader family will allow *all* family members to make informed decisions regarding their future in the family business. Many of these issues may have to be tabled more than once, so that each active family member has an opportunity to listen, understand and discuss them, with implications for the management and ownership of the business. The outcomes of these meetings should be summarized in writing for future reference. *Making a commitment to the family business meetings and the development of 'family business rules' addresses the #1 challenge in family business succession: communication, or the lack thereof!*

Ownership succession issues will impact the management succession plan and must be addressed at FBMs. The discussion and outcomes will allow active family members to make informed decisions regarding their future in the business, while outlining expectations. Sharing the outcomes with the broader family will inform them of the rules regarding the management succession process and what is being considered.

The management succession timeline will provide the planning horizon for the grooming of successors, who can acquire some of the requisite business skills and knowledge from the current (experienced) owners. The grooming plans are reviewed by the successor group and presented to the owners for review and approval. On transition, these plans and the roles and responsibilities of the current owners should meet the owners' expectations regarding the future management of the business, while allowing a smooth transition of control to the next generation.

Family Council Meetings (FCMs)

Family councils comprise the broader family: spouses, in-laws, children, grandparents, and grandchildren in the family business. These meetings are held annually or every couple of years, or more frequently, if the business is in a succession/transfer mode. The meetings should focus on informing family members of the "big picture," rather than day-to-day issues, and obtain feedback on family-based and business-based issues.

Setting up the Family Council

The owners of the family business should assign an active family member (or a non-active member with an active member as an assistant) to be the meeting coordinator or chairperson of the family council meetings, with rotation of the role among family members. This member will have access to business information that is of interest to the broader family and may need help in this role.

FCMs usually follow FBMs, wherein the tabled issues will have been discussed. The first FCMs may include a brief history of the family business, as a starting point. The participants must know what is expected of them, while being informed of how the business is doing, where it is headed and the role of the family in it.

Performance Reviews

Performance reviews should be an ongoing activity, and family members should be objective in their evaluations.

Stress in family relationships may be unfairly reflected in job evaluations. Non-family employees may be reluctant to provide negative reviews of family members.

Compensation for Family Members

Developing a compensation strategy for a family business can be challenging, but must be fair and representative of the value of work performed, and a top priority item for one of your family business meetings. Common problems include:

1. Managing Family Disagreements during the Succession Process: All family businesses experience disagreements or conflicts, which should be addressed as soon as they arise. A family business practitioner or a trusted unbiased third party can be very effective in mediating and finding common ground and resolution. Agreeing to a conflict resolution process is an important part of the family business rules.

2. Integrating the Family Component in Business Planning: Planning tends to be dominated by the owner(s), with little input from children (for fear of being disrespectful) and other members of management or outside advisers. This has often been cited as one of the major stumbling blocks in the management of the multi-generational family business enterprises.

Making Use of Outside Expertise

Most family businesses will retain the services of professional advisers such as accountants, lawyers, bankers, and insurance agents to assist the business as it evolves. Family businesses should also contact family business practitioners to assist them with their family business succession process: succession planning, strategic planning, and human resource management, while managing the impact of the family component on each of these business processes.

Management succession should precede the ownership succession process/plan. The details on how to manage family communication (family business meetings, family council meetings, and family business rules) and how to groom successors are outlined in the previous section, as part of the management succession activities.

Taking the Lead

As in the management succession process, the next generation of owners should take the lead in the ownership succession process by formulating the management and ownership succession strategies in consultation with, and with approval from, the owners, to provide both parties with the level of comfort needed to implement the succession plans.

Working through the succession plan between the owners and their trusted advisers without the active participation of the family often leads to unnecessary conflict. Regardless of who leads the process, it must be started. If you have next-generation family members working full-time in senior management positions, it's time to start the succession process.

Emotions and Their Impact

Transferring the ownership of any company can create a variety of emotions, ranging from guilt to freedom and happiness. The likelihood of a smooth transition will be significantly enhanced by family business meetings and family council meetings to address succession issues, in line with "generally accepted family business best practices." These meetings help manage family member expectations, while enabling them to make informed decisions about their future and providing sufficient comfort to implement the succession plans.

Ownership Succession Issues

The ownership succession issues to be addressed in your family business meetings include the following (also refer to the list of management succession issues in the previous section):

1. How will the family handle communication during this process (family business and council meetings and family business rules)?

2. What is the current thinking regarding the timeline for the ownership transition? Will it be a gradual transition? If so, when will it start and when will it be completed?

3. Who can own shares in the family business and why (active family members, non-active members, key employees, next-generation family members who may be interested in joining the business at a later date)? Which scenarios would give the current owners the most comfort? Which scenarios would give the next generation the most comfort?

4. How will the ownership transfer be funded? Will future owners be expected to invest personally in acquiring ownership via (for example) an upfront lump-sum payment? Are the current owners willing to have their value in the business paid over time through the profits of the company? What kind of assurances or collateral will the current owners need?

5. What will be the compensation arrangement for the owners after the transition? Will it be part of the transition price or will it be separate? How will it be determined?

6. What will be the compensation arrangement for the new owners? Will all of them be paid fair market value for the function each performs? Will bonuses be allocated based on ownership or performance, equally, or as a percentage of salary?

7. What role, if any, will the current owners play during and after the transition process?

8. At what stage of the ownership succession process will you communicate with the broader family and the employees, to what extent, and who will lead the communication process?

9. What will happen if an owner (current or future) becomes incapacitated, dies, or voluntarily decides to leave or retire from the ownership ranks of the business? What is the exit strategy?

10. What are the criteria for next-generation family members becoming owners? Who will determine the criteria and whether they have been met?

11. Do the owners have a current shareholders' agreement that reflects and supports the succession objectives/plan?

12. Do family members' wills (estate plans) support the succession plan?

13. Would a board of advisers benefit the next-generation owners?

The above ownership issues are best dealt with in the family business meetings with the active members, via the introduction of family business rules (which are then presented to the broader family at family council meetings) to guide the family members in the succession process. These meetings are the primary communication channels in the management of the family component during the succession process.

Governing the Family Component

Governance can be defined as the organizational structures that outline reporting responsibilities, combined with the organizational processes that determine how decisions are made. Corporate governance can include a board of directors and executive management committees with decision-making processes, such as board policies and operational manuals. Family businesses need to account for the family component via the family business meetings and family councils, and use the family business rules for decision making. Some large family businesses have established a "Family Office" to manage/govern their philanthropic activities.

Family businesses can have a board of directors or a board of advisers. A board of directors (BOD) has legal status and is responsible for overseeing the behavior and performance of the business. Incorporated businesses must hold at least one BOD meeting a year. Some family businesses will have a majority of non-family members on their BOD.

An advisory board, unlike a board of directors, has no legal status, formal power or legal liability for its actions. This board consists of a group of respected peers selected by the family business to offer advice on a number of business issues, including business strategy, executive compensation, and succession. Such a board can ensure a healthy, long-lived family business that will remain true to its mission and family values.

Minority Shareholders: Managing Expectations

Managing minority shareholders' expectations will help ensure family and business harmony. If the minority shareholders are active family members, they can discuss their expectations at business meetings. If not, this should be one of the agenda items for the family business meetings, to be shared subsequently at family council meetings and incorporated in a written policy on management of minority shareholders' expectations.

Shareholders' Agreement

An integral part of the succession plan is a shareholders' agreement, which formalizes the management and ownership succession plans and decisions made by the active family members during family business meetings. Family business rules developed during the succession process can be embodied or referenced in the shareholders' agreement, after working through the succession activities, since most of the issues will already have been decided.

Succession Self-Assessment Checklist

To help gauge succession readiness, review the self-assessment checklist below. (Bear in mind that family dynamics and family attributes vary between families and generations.)

1. *Creating a legacy*: Is it important to you and the next generation that the business stay within the family?

2. *Timing*: Have you established a timeline for the management and ownership succession processes? When should the process be started and should the

next-generation leaders and owners be in place? Has this been communicated to the next generation and the broader family?

3. *Comfort level*: Family issues and/or business issues will impact the future management and ownership of the business. As an owner and parent, are you doing anything to increase your comfort levels and minimize any potential negative impact on the family and the business?

4. *Options*: Are you are aware of your options? Do you know where to get the relevant information on the (identified) options so that you and the next generation of managers/owners can make informed decisions about your individual and collective futures in the family business?

5. *Communication*: Communication is the most important aspect of a successful transition. Decisions should be based on opinions expressed

by those who are affected by the succession process. Do you have a dedicated forum (i.e. family *business* meetings and family *council* meetings) that deals with succession issues and the succession process? Is there an active senior family member who is well suited to lead these meetings, and have you considered using an outside family business practitioner for this purpose?

6. *Expectations*: Can you clearly verbalize the expectations of your family members regarding their future roles/interests in the family business? How did you obtain this information?

7. *Guiding principles*: When transferring the management and ownership of a family business there are several options. Agreeing on some of the basics will help steer the process and manage family members' expectations. A formal process to discuss management and ownership succession

issues (i.e., family *business* meetings) that results in agreed-on succession principles can pave the way. Have you reflected on your guiding principles and discussed these with the active family members and the broader family? Consider the following:

- Employment: What are the criteria for the employment of family members? Can spouses and in-laws work in the business?

- Who can own: Will ownership be made available to non-active family members? If so, why, and what are their rights and expectations as non-active family owners? How will the active family members manage this issue (e.g., voting control)? Can spouses and in-laws become owners?

- Compensation: What is your current thinking regarding compensation for active family members and should it reflect market value?

- Leadership: Is there to be only one leader (e.g., president) or will co-leadership be entertained (e.g., co-presidents)? How will they be selected?

- Management succession: How do the management succession and ownership succession plans tie in and support one another? Is the ownership plan conditional on the management succession being in place, or will both plans be transferred at the same time? Will the ownership be held in trust until the management succession issues are addressed?

8. *Successor(s)*: Have you identified a successor(s)? Has this been communicated to the next generation?

Would the latter have selected the same individual(s)? How do you know?

9. *Changing role*: Have you thought through the kind of role you want to/should play during and after the management and ownership transition? Does the next generation support this role?

10. *Income security*: Is most of your disposable income tied up in the family business? Do you know how much you would need to draw from the family business after transitioning it to the next generation? Are you concerned about the security of your investment in the business after the transfer and is this preventing you from moving forward in the succession process?

11. *Who should lead*: Would you prefer that the next generation of managers/owners take the lead while obtaining your advice, support, and approval during the process or are you willing to take the lead?

12. *Managing conflict*: Is there an agreed-on process to deal with family conflict? Is it effective and agreed on by family members?

13. *Business strategy*: Is the next generation planning to take the business in the same direction that you would (growth, profits, and investments)? Has the next generation demonstrated its ability to do so?

14. *Exit strategy*: Will the shareholders' agreement for the next-generation owners include an exit strategy that is considered fair and amicable to all parties, while safeguarding the financial viability of the family business? Will it address incapacity, death, and voluntary retirement?

15. *Wills*: Does your will (estate plan) reflect and support your current thinking with respect to the future ownership of the family business? Is the next generation aware of this?

16. *Getting started*: Are you having trouble getting started? Can an outside family business adviser assist you in the succession process?

17. *Validation*: Would the next generation be in agreement with your answers to the above questions? How do you know?

Most family businesses do not complete their succession plan.

Sample Family Business Rules

Employment of Family Members

The owners of the family business encourage and support the participation of family members in the family business.

•　　　Employment of family members in the family business will be based on opportunity and merit. Compatibility of personalities will also be taken into consideration in assessing the employment and potential ownership of family members.

154

• Prior to an offer of employment being made to a family member (full- or part-time), the offer must be approved by all the owners.

• Family members aspiring to the ranks of management are expected to have the following qualifications:

– University/college degree (or equivalent)

– Three to five years of related work experience outside the family business

• Family members will be compensated on the basis of fair market value.

• A probationary period of six months will be applied to all new family members.

• Family members should preferably report to non-family members or to non-direct family members (i.e., not parents or siblings).

2. *Family Members Becoming Owners*

The owners are open to allowing active senior family members to be owners when they demonstrate their skills and commitment to the family business. Approval by the existing owners is required for a new family member to enter. In such cases, the company will carry out a "freeze": the current value of the company will be determined and distributed among the current owners in the ratio of their ownership interest in the form of "freeze" shares (or preferred shares), which the company must pay as per the agreed-on payment terms. At this time, a new class of ownership shares (common shares) will be distributed to the old and new owners. There is no price to pay for these new shares and subsequent growth of the business accrues equally to each of the owners, in proportion to shareholding. This process will be repeated as subsequent owners are accepted into the ownership ranks.

3. *Employment of Spouses and In-laws of Active Family Members*

The employment of spouses and in-laws of active family members in the family business is a delicate and sensitive issue. While not encouraged, this matter will be treated in the same manner as the employment of any family member outlined in policy #1 above.

4. *Executive Compensation*

Executive compensation for family members should be representative of the value of the work being performed, otherwise it may lead to conflicts.

5. *Exit Strategy*

The shareholders' agreement will provide for a fair and equitable exit strategy from the family business, on specific terms and conditions. Otherwise, the terms and conditions will be tabled and approved at a family business meeting and forwarded to legal counsel for future reference.

6. *Retirement Strategy*

In an effort to support the orderly transition of leadership and ownership in the family business among future generations, we propose a mandatory retirement date of 65 unless otherwise agreed to by the rest of the owners.

7. *Minority Shareholders*

The family business commits to informing all shareholders of their roles and responsibilities and what is expected of them. Minority shareholders will be kept informed of ownership type issues, including periodic business performance results. An annual distribution policy may be formulated.

8. *Conflict Resolution*

The purpose of a policy on conflict resolution is to provide active and non-active family members with a forum to discuss and resolve conflicts related to the family business. Family issues normally impact the business and business issues normally impact the family.

- The owners must establish a conflict management process to address conflict that is currently having or has the potential in the future to have a negative impact on the business. One of the owners will chair the process.

- The chair will schedule a meeting with the appropriate persons and conduct the meeting with the objective of facilitating the discussions and finding a resolution to the issue.

- The chair will consider using an outside facilitator (i.e., an expert in family business) to assist in dealing with the conflict.

- The chair will inform all family members of the existence of the conflict management process and how it operates.

9. *Prenuptial or Nuptial Agreements*:

The purpose of a prenuptial or nuptial agreement is to safeguard the ownership/control shares of the family business so that in the event of a marriage breakup the ownership structure is not inappropriately altered, put at risk, or compromised. Therefore, the following policy is endorsed by the owners.

- As a condition of ownership in the family business, the owner is required to conclude a prenuptial or nuptial agreement in a form acceptable to the company's corporate solicitor.

- Any family member planning to join the ownership ranks of the family business is encouraged to conclude a prenuptial agreement.

10. *Family Trusts and Other Trusts*

Each owner must ensure, in a form acceptable to the company's corporate lawyer, that his or her family trusts or other trusts support the terms and conditions of the shareholders' agreement with regard to rights and privileges.

11. *Leaves of Absence and Sabbaticals*

There must be a policy regarding leaves of absence and sabbaticals. This will enable family business owners to succeed in their roles as parents, boss, and owners.

•   Sabbaticals are intended to accommodate extended leaves for the sake of, for example, continued education, health reasons, or special circumstances.

•   Entitlement is based on having worked at least three years in the family business.

•   The employee's current position, or one comparable to it, is to be provided on their return.

- The leave is without pay, unless otherwise determined by the owners.

- If the leave is for educational purposes, costs may be reimbursed on successful completion of the program.

- The approval of all the owners is required.

Leaves of Absence

- Leaves of absence are intended to comprise short periods of time (i.e., weeks to months) to allow family members to deal with short-term illnesses or personal issues.

- The leave is generally with pay.

- Entitlement is based on assessing each individual case, for which the approval of all the owners is required.

12. *Business Loans to Family Members*: Purchasing Goods/Services from Family Members

The family business may experience requests from active and non-active family members for personal loans. If not consistently handled, these situations can cause long-lasting conflict among the owners and family.

•   All requests for personal business loans or other financial transactions with family members must be approved by a unanimous vote of the owners, with the terms and conditions of the transaction agreed to being confirmed in writing. This would include:

–   The full amount of the loan, commitment, or other financial transaction

–   Precisely to whom it is being lent or committed

–   The proposed payment schedule and any related interest

–   What happens in case of default

–   Whether the loans should be insured

13. *Philanthropy / Charity*

The family business will develop a strategy on charitable giving to be reviewed and approved by all the owners.

−   Which charities we want to support and why.

−   What amount we are prepared to donate annually. This should be budgeted.

−   The name in which the funds are being donated (the family business, individuals).

14. *Public Relations*

The owners will decide who will be appointed to represent them in the media and in communication with the general public. All requests for written or oral statements by the media or general public, public appearances and any other public relations activities will be channeled to and handled by the company representative(s).

15. *Conflict of Interest*

Each family member must ensure that he or she is not in conflict of interest while employed in the family business. Any family member who is unsure must table the situation at an executive meeting for review.

• A family member employed in the family business will be considered in conflict of interest if he or she has engaged either directly or indirectly in any related business activities without the consent of the other owners.

• No family member employed in the family business may engage in any other active business without the unanimous consent of the owners.

16. *Changes to the Family Business Rules*

Changes to the family business rules require the majority vote of the active owners. Changes will be presented to the broader family at the next family council meeting.

CHAPTER 6 – How Does One Thrive in a Home-based Business?

Lack of motivation among employees seems to be a universal problem, resulting from the inadequate leadership and management skills of many leaders, managers and supervisors, who do not seem to understand that employees are business partners who need to be motivated via ethical leadership: respect, caring, sharing, challenging assignments, etc. A reasonable compensation package, combined with praise, fair criticism, challenging assignments and other factors do not guarantee loyalty to the business and low employee turnover! Many employees, having faced repeated disappointments, feel the need to combat this problem by starting out on their own, with a view to independence, financial freedom, flexible hours and the freedom to make decisions that could increase their own wealth, rather than their boss's. However, frustration with one's boss does not justify starting one's own business, which calls for a great degree of business knowledge and discipline and must be preceded by careful thought and planning, especially in the case of a home-based business. In addition, one needs to be able to set up and control budgets and spending, while establishing financial goals and being able to "roll with the punches" when things do not go according to plan. There are times when you will have to work alone, without anyone to talk to or liaise with. Spare time must be used constructively.

Technical expertise alone does not guarantee business success! Many business organizations close down in the early years, thus confirming the need for (ethical) leadership and marketing skills, in addition to technical skills. Prior to starting off on one's own, one is advised to attend courses on the leadership, management and planning aspects of business. In addition, one has to learn from the mistakes of one's former supervisors and managers and treat employees as precious investments, in an ethical manner. This will ensure their loyalty while contributing to personal as well as (profitable) corporate growth.

Before starting out on your own, ensure that you have a set of skills that are in demand and a reasonable amount of cash to tide you over during lean periods of business. Many businesses fail because of a shortage of cash for assets or expenses. A line of credit or credit card(s) can come in handy, but you must ensure that the cost of borrowing is justified by the income generated as a result of borrowing. You must believe in yourself and be positive and persistent. Do not be unduly influenced by tempting advertisements on television, in the press or elsewhere for products or services that appear to be appealing, cheap and easy to re-sell at a profit. Engage in thorough research before embarking on a project or a series of projects.

A home-based business may be geared towards providing supplemental income and eventually replacing one's full-time job, or it may be an attempt to supplement retirement income if life throws a curve ball during retirement. An action plan based on marketable skills must be accompanied by a willingness to put in a concerted effort to achieve one's goals.

Forming and Naming the Business

If you decide to operate as a sole proprietorship, your liability will be unlimited: if your business assets are insufficient to settle your debts, your creditors can proceed against your personal assets. Adequate insurance policies can protect you, but insurance companies are not really inclined to settle claims in a way that satisfies creditors. Therefore, you can either make up the shortfall or protect yourself from the outset, by incorporating (with limited liability) and considering the possibility of closing your corporation and starting a new one if customers or creditors are unreasonable in their demands.

As far as naming the business is concerned, it is not advisable to use your own name, either because the business enterprise is a separate entity, as distinct from yourself, or because you may wish to sell your business at a future date, without selling your name, with implications for goodwill attached to your personal name. Use a name that suits the business operation.

Setting up the Business

Setting up your home-based business will have implications for your privacy and your family life. Communicate with your family and ensure that you spend quality time with them, giving them their space, adequate telephone usage, confidentiality regarding the presence of family, friends, neighbors, disturbances and so on. You must also consider zoning (which you may be able to dispute and ask for a variance based on your specific circumstances: type of business, low volume of customers, no noise, no environmental hazards, etc.), dedicating space exclusively for business, storage, parking for customers and others, signage, telephone lines, utilities, insurance, tax implications regarding allowable deductions, and other factors.

Establish a healthy relationship with a bank that is known for good service and is geared towards helping businesses such as yours while being quite flexible in approach. Ensure that the appropriate licenses are in place to enable you to operate legally and efficiently. You may choose to have a logo that identifies your business and promotes effective advertising.

The Business Plan

A business plan may not be essential to success, but it does help provide a blueprint that can be adjusted, if necessary. A business plan outlines the history of the business, its nature and purpose, short-, medium- and long-term goals, the target market and characteristics, market research conducted, competitive strategy and related matters, and includes financial statements to show where the business is expected to be headed over the next (for example) three years.

Operations, Technology and Related Matters

Some businesses can operate from a corner of a room – others cannot! Be aware of your situation and set up your office accordingly, bearing in mind space requirements, storage, number and frequency of customers, neat appearance of the office and surrounding area, lighting, the floor, furniture, feng shui, hygiene factors, cleaning, mail services, filing, bookshelves, zoning, parking, entrance, greeting customers and related factors.

As far as technology is concerned, ensure that you have good quality telephones, an efficient computer with suitable software and easy, fast access to the Internet.

Technology must be complemented by excellent customer service.

Buying an Existing Business

If you are considering buying a business, be careful when valuing it. Review the financial statements for the past few years, review the credibility of the accountant and take into account location, market share, growth rate, assets, liabilities and undisclosed items, such as obsolete inventories or inventories held but not paid for, pending lawsuits, possible goodwill. Ensure that the agreement of sale prevents the current owner from competing with you for a certain specified period of time and within a certain radius of your location. Interview existing employees and discuss your acquisition plans with them. Distribute questionnaires to ascertain what current employees like and dislike about the company you are hoping to acquire.

The Importance of a Good Lawyer, Accountant and Others

A home-based business, like any other business, needs a good lawyer, a good accountant and a good insurance company, for obvious reasons. It also helps to have a healthy relationship with a bank that is quite flexible in approach. Liability insurance, workers' compensation, business interruption insurance, health, dental, medical and disability insurance, property insurance, auto insurance and related matters should also be taken into consideration.

Communication and Business Dealings

You must stay organized and communicate well with insiders and outsiders, such as customers, suppliers, the bank, the government and others. Be careful in your dealings with people and also note that you will be busier at certain times of the day. Communication face to face, over the phone, via e-mail messages and letters should be courteous and effective. Pay yourself reasonably for the services you provide – *you are not working for your business for free!*

Stay focused and motivated, be creative, attend training courses and business events, join volunteer organizations and look for lines of business that complement your own business. Promote yourself at all times, whether you are attending a function or merely visiting a mall, but do not appear to be desperately in need of business. Your communication skills must impress people, so that they want to do business with you. Advertising helps, but it must be complemented by excellent service and follow-up. *People are attracted to successful businessmen, rather than those who are depressed and needy – always bear this in mind.*

When you are unproven and starting a business or changing careers, working for free or offering one free service or session is an effective way of gaining experience and business connections.

CHAPTER 7 – Retirement – A New Haven?

Before retiring, one must live within one's means, e.g., pay off credit card balances within the grace period to eliminate interest charges, buy gas at self-service rather than full-service gas stations, and invest at least 10% of one's income wisely, while paying oneself first. Emergency funds are necessary when faced with expenses that are not covered by insurance or to take advantage of excellent bargains.

Consider the impact of the following categories of expenditure that may drain one's financial resources during retirement:

a) Medical expenses due to the age factor;

b) Long-term care expenses, because more women have joined the work force and are therefore unable to attend to their elderly parents;

c) Heating expenses, unless one will move to a warmer climate; and

d) Leisure and travel activities.

Possible sources of income during the retirement period include consulting, as a popular form of entrepreneurism, and property management.

Qualified retirement plans include IRAs and Keoghs in the USA, Registered Savings Plans (RSPs) in Canada, and company-sponsored savings programs. Some insurance policies are treated as tax shelters, in the sense that certain withdrawals from them are considered to be withdrawals of principal and, therefore, non-taxable. A tax shelter is any investment that enables a taxpayer to claim a deduction, loss or tax credit, that can offset income from other sources. When it comes to investment income from real estate, mutual funds and other financial instruments, be aware of all the deductions that you are entitled to and put as much income in the name of the lower income-earning spouse!

Government benefits and government pension plans can be diminished by post-retirement income and assets. In Canada, you may continue to work beyond the age of 65 and avail yourself of unemployment benefits if dismissed in accordance with the rules for unemployment benefits.

Employee Benefit Plans

Understanding a business enterprise's retirement package may be extremely difficult, but this hurdle must be overcome if one is to benefit from the latter package. The tax implications of such packages, together with incentives for early retirement, should be discussed with one's accountant prior to any decision being taken. Moreover, one has to check the reputation and integrity of the business enterprise in question. Consider the following:

1. Defined Benefit Plans, whereby the firm sets aside money for the employee's retirement, based on a formula that takes into account years of service, salary and other relevant factors. Payment may be a lump sum or monthly installments, but the tax effects should be considered prior to withdrawal.

2. Defined Contribution Plans, whereby the firm matches the employee's contribution via an agreed percentage or share of profits. Alternatively, the employee may participate in a stock ownership program, whereby the employer matches the employee's purchase of stock, at an agreed percentage. Defined Contribution Plans are portable and normally vest quicker than (1) above; these plans may even be incorporated within (say) a 401K salary reduction program. Beware of small

179

businesses where a few executives receive higher benefits than other employees.

Other Investment Plans

(1) *An individual's house.* An individual's home may provide his main source of security, with some property expenses being tax allowable. Capital Gains Taxes can normally be deferred on sale of the house as long as they are rolled over into a new house within the tax allowable period. After a certain age, a stipulated portion of the profits from the sale of the house may not be taxable. You may consider selling your house and moving to a smaller one, renting an apartment, or taking a mortgage against the equity (i.e. reverse mortgage your house and buying a tax-free annuity such that the mortgage can be repaid on death of both spouses and sale of the house). In Canada, the sale of one's principal residence does not incur any tax liability.

Moreover, real estate can be a good investment if rented to good tenants with rental income exceeding mortgage payments and maintenance costs. Even if you do not rent out part of your house, your mortgage payments should take into account rent otherwise payable, thereby reducing the net cost of your house. A 15-year amortization period may be advisable, but make sure to shop around for the best interest rates and consider borrowing from relatives and offering them tax-free income. Buy at a good price and near water, if possible, with access to transportation, shopping and schools. You are advised to review *The Smith Manoeuvre*, which can help in wealth creation.

In some cases, it may be cheaper to rent (rather than buy) and invest the difference in mutual funds, for example, to provide a higher retirement income.

(2) *Qualified investment/savings plans* will generate income that is not taxable, but there are penalties for early withdrawal. These plans may incorporate suitable mutual funds. A mutual fund is a professionally managed pool of

money. Diversify further by investing in international mutual funds with sound long-term performance records. Mutual fund income is taxable, but the balance can be reinvested. Capital gains are taxable on disposal of the mutual funds in question, but the formalities involved in encashment may discourage one from reducing one's portfolio of mutual funds.

Government programs may provide a source of income during retirement but there are specific rules that have to be followed in order to benefit from these.

Life insurance policies can provide a source of income during retirement, but these policies should be considered a last resort, as far as income is concerned, unless one can withdraw cash without tax consequences or one is terminally ill. Life insurance provides financial protection against lost income, debt (including mortgage and taxes), and estate management expenses, including funeral expenses, education and inflation faced by your loved ones.

Disability insurance policies protect earning power and help cover expenses during disability (own or any occupation, indexed for inflation, waiver of premium, non-cancellable, benefit period after a certain period, percentage of income as disability coverage), and may help an individual retire before the normal age of retirement, if he or she cannot work at his own occupation.

Estate Planning

Plan your estate carefully, with the help of a suitable financial planner. Joint ownership and children are no substitute for a well-drafted will and an efficient and trustworthy executor. You may need to draft a power of attorney with the help of a good lawyer and review your will at specific intervals or as circumstances change. Give a copy of recent wills to an effective lawyer-executor, together with a statement of net assets and relevant documents; otherwise the government will distribute your estate in accordance with the law. A will may have a clause that mentions something like, "any beneficiary who attempts to dispute the contents of this will can and will lose his share of the estate and this portion will be donated to …. Charity." You may donate to your favorite charity, so long as you follow the guidelines set by the tax authorities.

If your heirs are very young, you may set up a trust through an attorney/lawyer to hold property for them, with precise instructions regarding the management of such property.

Proper estate planning will help reduce or eliminate estate taxes, depending on the circumstances. Your estate should be sufficiently liquid to avoid the sale of its assets at knock-down/fire sale prices. Executors should prepare in advance for the task of executing their client's will, by discussing with their clients regarding their financial affairs, intentions, location of inventories, records, will and related matters. Managing the client's estate includes distribution, record-keeping, filing claims and related matters.

CHAPTER 8 – Insurance and Other Financial Matters: A Conceptual Approach

Introduction

In this section we shall look at the subject of life insurance, disability insurance, critical illness insurance, long-term care insurance, mutual funds, segregated funds, retirement and related matters (mainly) in a Canadian context. Needs analysis is of paramount importance.

(a) Living Needs include: disability and critical illness coverage, medical, extended health care, long-term care, education for children through RESPS and (perhaps) Universal Life Insurance policies.

(b) On death, we are concerned with probate and estate taxes, debts (including mortgage and credit cards, loans, etc.), funeral expenses, survivor's income, and the education of children.

Permanent needs include funeral costs, estate taxes, survivor's income, and estate creation for loved ones/charities. Younger people are interested in wealth accumulation: older people are interested in estate protection.

Unilateral Contract: where only one party can change the terms e.g. face value + utmost good faith + printed contract which cannot be negotiated/altered + aleatory: policy owner knows what the insurance company will do but the latter does not know what the former will do.

Term Insurance (usually until age 80) covers temporary risks of a known duration and may be

(1) Renewable without a medical examination, but premiums increase, in accordance with the schedule

187

of the original policy. It may be cheaper to take a new policy from the same or another company or to be medically examined, if one is healthy.

(2) Convertible Insurance can convert to permanent insurance before a specified age without a medical examination, e.g. if you are uncertain about the future, as in the case of a newly married couple, or you cannot afford permanent insurance at this point in time. Premiums are based on age.

(3) Non-renewable insurance requires a new application and medical examination.

(4) Mortgage insurance: no medical + higher premiums + policy ends when you sell the house.

Term premium = f(Mortality Cost + Company's Operating Margin + Investment Returns + Tax)

Mortality table: life expectancy based on age, gender, smoking/non-smoking and region e.g. North America.

(Mortality) cost of insurance: Net Amount at Risk x Probability of Death = (e.g.) 100,000 x 0.122% (Mortality Table for Age 30 years)) = 100,000 x 0.122/100 = $122.

Operating margin/policy fee: covers sales commissions, underwriting costs, medicals, rent, salaries, utilities, etc. and profits...say $6 per policy.

Higher Investment Returns mean lower premiums. Tax at 6% is charged by each province to insurance companies.

The rating of policies is based on medical conditions (unless diabetes, etc.), smoking, family history, etc.

Term to 100 Policies: a cheap permanent policy when not interested in cash value, e.g. donation. You must pay premiums until the age of 100 and your beneficiary will receive a benefit whether you die before or after reaching the age of 100 years.

Grace Period: if you die during this 31-day period, beneficiary gets death benefit – o/s premium.

Lapse: If the grace period of 31 days is exceeded, the policy remains dormant for 2 years, but can be re-instated upon payment of outstanding premiums + penalties + re-instatement costs + medical examination. The premium is based on original age, but adjusted if the insured person's health deteriorates or if he or she becomes a smoker during the grace/dormant period. The incontestability and suicide exclusion clause start again and the company can refuse to re-instate the policy, based on factors such as medical conditions.

Incontestability Clause

(a) Non-material Misrepresentation: the insurance company has 2 years (same as for the suicide clause) from the actual policy date to investigate and correct the application.

(b) Material Misrepresentation ≠ *misstatement of age (reduced death benefit)* and the policy can be cancelled. If the material misrepresentation is intentional, the company can prosecute for fraud,

Whole Life Insurance (WL) covers long-term risks and taxes upon death and there are insurance as well as investment components, with no premiums being paid beyond the age of 100 years, because the investment value should exceed the face value of the policy. Premiums are higher than for Universal Life (UL) policies, because investments are more conservative. Adjustable WL has lower premiums than guaranteed WL, but UL is still cheaper.

The owner of the policy can pay more than the stipulated premium and build cash value, which can be used to buy a paid-up policy, if and when the owner finds it difficult to pay the stipulated premium. You may choose to buy a limited pay WLI policy and pay for a specified number of years, as guaranteed by the company.

Adjusted cost basis (ACB): Actual Cost of insurance or investment with after-tax dollars = Premiums - the Cost of Pure Insurance - the dividends in par WL policies

Policy Reserve: $ growth within insurance policy.

Insurance proceeds during life: Policy Growth = CSV – ACB is taxable in full, as income, whether loan e.g. 90% x CSV or not … when you repay loan, same excess can be used to reduce taxable income. Death benefit will be reduced by the unpaid loan and interest.

Insurance proceeds upon death are tax free to beneficiary.

Account value: Balance in your account, but insurance company may deduct a surrender charge.

Owner: The insured may or may not be the life insured but must have an insurable interest: self, spouse, child, step-child, grandchild, partner, employee, person being funded by Mr. X has an insurable interest in Mr. X or anyone who signs a document stating insurable interest in him or her, subject to company's approval.

Transferring the Ownership of a Policy

If there is a transfer to one's spouse (i.e. lived with him or her for ≥ 12 months or parent of one's child), child, step-child, grandchild or parent, then no taxes are payable. The ACB remains the same as that of the original owner.

Other Transfers: tax implications to owner @ Account Value – ACB = taxable income

Transfer to Charity: (i) Donation receipt for CSV of donated policy or (ii) Donation receipt for premiums paid on a donated policy.

Non-forfeiture Benefits

If you do not pay your premiums, they can be paid via an automatic premium loan (APL) through the cash surrender value (CSV). When the CSV runs out, the grace period will begin and if there is lapse of more than 31 days, you have to review what was mentioned above. Options include having a Reduced Face Amount of Policy or the CSV can be used to buy a term policy of less than or equal to the original face amount, without conversion rights.

Participating Whole Life Policies

Premiums payable may be higher than for non-participating policies, but if the insurance company makes a profit because of reduced costs/higher investment returns, the excess premiums are called policy dividends. These are different from corporate dividends, and are used to lower subsequent premiums, invested in accordance with the policy owner's instructions, or to buy an additional paid-up policy or a one-year term policy without a medical examination, *depending on the contract.* Such amounts reduce the ACB. If premiums are less than what should have been charged, the insurance company takes the hit.

Universal life insurance policies are flexible or unbundled. The owner can change the face amount, premiums, frequency, and even the life insured and there is a guaranteed death benefit. The policy reserve of the WL policy is called the investment account of the UL policy and can be used to invest in GICs, stocks, and even mutual funds, *but not in segregated funds.*

Insurance charge = Cost of Insurance as for Term 100 + Policy Fee + Tax;

Insurance Option: level term or Annual Renewable Term (ART) – can be switched to level term within the agreed period;

Grace period = 31 days, with lapse rules as discussed earlier;

Death benefit options: level death benefit/face amount or level death benefit + account value or indexed at agreed percentage or COLA or level death benefit + accumulated gross premiums.

In WL policies, you only receive a level death benefit option.

Withdrawals: excess over ACB is taxable income; e.g. if ACB = $30,000 and Account Value = $40,000, then 75% of the withdrawal is taxable income.

Beneficiaries

The beneficiary will receive the death benefit tax free, but revocable beneficiaries can be changed e.g. through a will.

If the beneficiary is irrevocable e.g. owner's estate/other beneficiary, then written consent is needed for any changes e.g. loans, cashing in the policy, or transfer of ownership.

The death benefit is tax free and payable in accordance with the owner's instructions (lump sum, installments, annuity, interest only) and is creditor proof when a beneficiary is named in the policy, otherwise the death benefit goes to the estate. During life, CSV is creditor proof if the beneficiary is irrevocable or a preferred class beneficiary: spouse, child, step-child, grandchild or grandparent.

If the owner and the beneficiary die simultaneously, the latter is considered to have died first and the death benefit goes to the owner's estate.

Accelerated Death Benefits, Supplementary Benefits and Riders

Living benefits to life insured: Accelerated Death Benefit (ADB) ≤ 50% of death benefit to life insured upon terminal illness; critical illness – waiting period ≤ 30 days for terminal illness and long-term care when ≥ 2 of the following apply: unable to toilet, unable to dress, needs constant supervision, or mentally ill. These benefits per contract will reduce the death benefit.

Disability benefits rider: If disabled per *own* occupation, then the benefit will be payment after 31 days and up to 24 months.

Waiver of Premium: if life insured is totally disabled per *own* occupation, the insurance company will pay premiums after the elimination period and refund premiums paid during the elimination period, but the Payer Disability rider is applicable for the disability of the owner.

Parent Waiver: when the life insured is a minor.

Dread disease rider: diseases listed in the policy – amount paid is deducted from death benefit, as for long-term care rider, but different for a critical illness rider.

Term insurance rider: The family coverage rider is only applicable to the spouse, children between the ages of 14 days and 21 years (or 23 years if studying at an accredited educational institution), even if you do not inform the company of the newborn child. If the life insured dies, the spouse can convert the rider to permanent insurance ≤31 days of death.

Guaranteed insurance rider: covers up to 50% of the face amount of the policy and can be bought when offered by the company, without a medical examination, but additional insurance will bear premium according to the age at conversion.

ADD: double indemnity or twice the face amount of death benefit for accidental death or dismemberment, as defined by the insurance company.

Paid-up additions rider: an extra lump sum payment can expedite the paying-up of the policy.

Upon the Death of a Person

Estate: Assets are valued at fair market value (FMV) and liabilities are frozen/crystallized in the estate. No capital gains on main residence, death benefit and lottery winnings. Income tax on income to death. RSPs are considered withdrawn and taxable unless rolled over to a spouse and there is a probate tax @1.5% x estate value.

You must pay taxes to the Canada Revenue Agency and get a clearance certificate from the Canada Revenue Agency. Then the executor pays creditors and the balance is distributed in accordance with the will. If there is no will, provincial family law will apply.

How Much Insurance to Sell?

(a) Capitalization of Income Method: Annual

Income/Real Rate of Interest = 50,000/85-2% (e.g.)

= $833,333.

(b) Capital Retention Method: considers assets and

liabilities, *while realizing that some assets will not be sold*

upon death of first spouse:

(i) Assets:	Death Benefit	$2,500
	Investments	$200,000
	Cash	$80,000
	Home	
	Cottage	
	TOTAL	$282,500.
(ii) Final Expenses:	Funeral	$20,000
	Legal and Accounting	$ 10,000
	Taxes	$150,000

Home	
Cottage	
Mortgage	$500,000
Debts	$30,000
Total Final Expenses	$710,000

Cash Need = 710K – 282.5K = 427.5K

(iii) Income Needs

	Husband Dies	Wife Dies
Total Annual Income	53,400	108,400
Total Annual Expenses	61,000	61,000
Difference	- 7,600	47,400
Assumption: Interest Rate	6%	6%
F/Interest Rate	-126,667(G)	
Insurance Need	-554,167	-427,500

The insurance contract must be in writing and include the application plus all documents written so far; the death benefit may be payable via a lump sum or installments/interest only until a specified age or a life annuity may be specified, depending on what the owner chooses. If the owner does not specify this, the beneficiary can do so.

The agent must witness the owner's and the life insured's signature on the application, which also asks for permission to access the MIB database (set up by insurance companies and including medical and other info, e.g. driving offences in North America of anyone who has applied for insurance coverage). If you answer "No" to all questions on the temporary insurance agreement, i.e. diseases, medical procedures and driving violations, and if you are younger than 65, the agent will collect the first premium and provide coverage of up to 500K for 90 days or less, but subject to cash or check encashment. If the owner dies within 90 days, the underwriter will check the answers, and if they are acceptable the death benefit will be paid.

The insurance company must ensure an insurable interest, the need for insurance, the financial ability to pay premiums, health and necessary medical tests (by the company's doctor, i.e. an attending physician statement, if necessary), MIB info, motor vehicle report, etc. and possible inspections regarding lifestyle, drugs, and other matters, by an investigative agency appointed by the insurance company on any project.

Claims Process

The beneficiary must present the life insured's death certificate, proof of age (usually birth certificate) and the beneficiary's claim form. The claim will normally be settled within 90 days.

Disability insurance coverage is available to full-time employees (Morbidity≠ Mortality tables) and provides for a replacement of income for disability through injury (mandatory) or mental/physical sickness (optional) but may be subject to a medical examination if applying for the sickness element. The insurance benefit covers salary, commissions, net research grants and net business income, usually between 60 and 70 % of income, but not exceeding $5,000. This type of insurance coverage is important for self-employed individuals, because they do not have any workers' compensation or unemployment insurance and their Canada pension plan disability coverage is limited.

Disability is defined as the inability to perform substantial functions of one's job. The insured must need supervision by a physician. *The definition of disability varies between firms, and the insurance company can cancel the policy unless the policy is guaranteed non-cancellable. Moreover, if the policy is guaranteed renewable, the terms can be changed by the insurance company only if they change the terms for the class/category of people.* If premiums are .paid with after-tax dollars, the disability benefits are tax-free. If the insured is less than 65 years of age, disability coverage is more important than life coverage, because of the probability of becoming disabled, as compared with the probability of dying before the age of 65.

Disability insurance on the basis of one's "own occupation" is suited to professionals. If you cannot perform the important duties of work at your own occupation e.g., a surgeon is not allowed to operate if he or she has a wound,, you will receive the disability benefit.

Disability insurance on the basis of one's "regular occupation" is suited to middle management and skilled/office workers. If you cannot perform the important duties of your occupation and do not work elsewhere, the coverage *may* pay the shortfall in income. Disability insurance on the basis of "any occupation" is suited to non-skilled workers.

If the loss of income is greater than or equal to 80% i.e. residual disability, the policy can cover the full disability benefit. (These variables are illustrated in the table on the following page.)

Variables in a Disability Policy

Presumptive disability: Permanent loss of 2 limbs, sight, speech, hearing, paralysis or paraplegia (paralyzed on one side). This coverage (*not offered in group disability policies*) offers the full benefit even if you work and get paid.

	Own Occupation	**Regular Occupation**	**Any Occupation**
	Highest Premium	*Lower premium*	*Lowest Premium*
One Hand Crushed	√	√	√
Treatment re: Twisted Hand	√	√	x (because
			he can do some other job)
Work as a Consultant	√	x	x
Return to Original Occupation	x	x	x

√ = Will receive disability insurance benefit

Benefit period: For how long do you wish to be paid the disability benefit: 6 months / 1 year / 5 years for each disability occurrence, or to age 65 or 70 (unless you have the lifetime extension benefit to cover you until recovery or death)? Most people recover within one year, unless the case is extreme, so it is practical to have disability coverage for 1 year.

Elimination Period: The waiting period for each disability before benefits kick in. This can be longer where the employee has WSIB coverage. For policies with an 'accumulation of days' feature, consider previous waiting periods.

Recurrent Disability clause: If the second occurrence of disability is from the same/related cause and occurs within the period specified in the contract (say ≤ 6 months) of the original disability, then it will be considered to be a continuation of the original disability, i.e. there will not be a new waiting period.

Partial Disability clause: When you cannot perform all your functions all the time or when you are recovering from total disability which is expected not to exceed 6 months.

Residual Disability (partial, but for a longer period): If you are totally disabled (own/regular/any) for the contractual qualification period and you partially recover, then residual disability benefit applies, in accordance with the contract. For example, consider the case of a machine operator who earns $4,000 per month, with disability coverage of $2,000 per month, who crushes one of his or her hands, rendering him or her totally disabled for 6 months. He then recovers and gets a new job for $3,000 per month. If he or she has residual disability, he or she will receive a benefit of 25% x Disability Coverage ($2,000) per month = $500 per month. *If the loss is less than 20% the benefit will be nil, but if the loss exceeds 80%, the full residual benefit will be paid.*

The premium will be based on occupation (professionals and skilled workers), but pre-existing conditions will not be covered.

There will be no disability coverage for injury resulting from intentional acts or attempted suicide, drugs, war, impaired driving, pregnancy (unless complications prevent either spouse from working), AIDS or HIV, cosmetic surgery within 6 months of the policy being issued, mistakes during surgery, and certain other factors.

Various Riders/Disability Policies: These riders provide coverage for accidental death and dismemberment (ADD), lifetime benefits extension and coverage after the age of 65, etc.

Concurrent disability applies to disability from more than one injury or sickness, e.g. a driving accident causes sickness and injury, in which case only one month's disability benefit will be paid. Pre-existing conditions *may* be covered with a limited payment or an extended waiting period.

There are several types of disability policies and riders.

Guaranteed non-cancellable rider: the insurer cannot change anything;

Guaranteed Renewable: the insurer can change the premium for a particular class of people;

Conditionally Renewable: the insurer can renew the policy under certain conditions;

Optionally Renewable: the policy is renewable at the owner's option;

Cancellable: the insurer can cancel the policy at any time, with at least 15 days' notice.

Disability income is not taxable if you pay the premiums or if the employer pays and includes the amount on your T4.

Riders: Waiver of Premium, ADB (lump sum tax free), AD&D (lump sum tax free), COLA for inflation but not deflation, own occupation rider for (say) 5 years, etc.

Extended Health Care

If medical coverage provided by the government (OHIP) is insufficient to cover medical care, extended health care can cover the shortfall. This is tax-free regardless of who pays the premiums and there is a 10-day rescission period. Premiums are based on the risk attaching to each class and the terms include renewability, grace period, claims and procedures. *Over-insurance is prohibited.*

Employment Insurance

Taxable disability benefits are payable, after deducting WSIB and group disability benefits. Such benefits cover unemployment and some disabilities, but you must have worked for at least 600 hours. The elimination period is 14 days and the benefit period is 15 weeks, with payment equal to 55% of insurable earnings, up to $42,100. The maximum benefit is $400 per week, minus deductions at source.

Canada Pension Plan (CPP)

Taxable disability benefits are payable if the disability is *severe and prolonged* and you must have contributed to CPP in 4 of the last 6 years. The elimination period is 4 months and the benefit is available up to the age of 65.

Dependents of up to 18 years old, or up to the age of 25 years and studying full-time, and eligible disabled pensioners may receive a monthly CPP disability.

WSIB – Tax-free Disability Benefits

These disability benefits cover work-related accidents and industrial illnesses for up to 90% of eligible earnings. This includes prescriptions, medical treatment, rehabilitation, training, special clothing, and attendant care. A death benefit by way of a lump sum plus monthly benefits is payable if the employee dies within twelve months of an accident or an industrial illness. *Workmen's compensation is tax free.*

Accident and Sickness Insurance

This benefit covers disability and medical requirements beyond OHIP prescription drugs, dental (comprehensive), vision, and emergency travel health.

Critical Illness (Living Benefit)

This benefit applies to life-threatening cancer, heart attack, stroke, coronary artery, bypass surgery, AIDS on the job and some other medical problems. The survival period is normally at least 30 days, depending on the type of critical illness. There can be a return of premium rider to get a *tax-free* refund of premiums if there is no claim during the policy period. The policy can be a standalone policy or by way of a rider on a life insurance policy. Pre-existing conditions are *not* covered.

Long-term Care Insurance (LTC)

This coverage applies if you cannot perform any two of the following functions: eating, bathing, dressing, toileting, moving or if you suffer from cognitive impairment or mental illness. You can receive benefits of up to $10,000 per month, but only those aged 40-80 years can be insured for LTC. The buyer of the policy must be between the ages of 16 and 80 e.g. a grandson can buy a policy for his grandparent who needs constant care. The benefit is paid to a professional/institution for charges incurred.

Group Insurance – one-year term on all types of group policies.

We have looked at individual policies. Now let us review group policies, where a group is defined to include a company, partnership, association, club, sole proprietor with employees, and some other organizations. The emphasis is on the employee's income, job, hours of work, whether the employee smokes or not and some other factors, but not on age or medical factors. The owner controls the policy and can customize it.

If the group consists of at least 25 members, there is no medical requirement.

Contribution plan: the employee contributes to premiums and may have a waiver of premium benefit with a 90-day elimination period.

Non-contribution plan: where the employer pays 100% of the premium.

There are two systems: non-refund/retention accounting and refund accounting, where excess premiums are refunded to the company. Larger companies usually prefer the latter system.

Instead of buying a group insurance policy, the company may settle claims directly, i.e. take self-insurance and retain the services of an insurance company to administer the policy, for a fee.

Premium Rates

Experience rates are used by large companies, whereas manual or book rates are used by small companies and blended rates (manual with an adjustment) are used by medium-sized groups.

Basic coverage is available without a medical examination but additional coverage normally requires a medical examination.

This type of policy can be converted into an individual policy within 31 days of leaving the group and without a medical examination, with the rate of premium being based on age, health, and some other factors. The benefit is tax-free. For an individual policy, in the case of a misstatement of age, the death benefit will be according to actual age, less additional premiums that should have been paid if age was understated. For group life insurance, only the premium will be adjusted. The benefit may include an additional amount to help the surviving spouse for a short term after the first spouse's death.

Group Disability Insurance

If a group policy pays a benefit, the employment insurance (EI) and CPP disability benefits will be reduced. If the group policy is better than the EI policy, the company will receive a discount on EI premiums. If the employer pays the premium and does not declare it on the employee's T4 slip, the employee is taxable for the disability benefit.

Short-term disability is that of up to 17 weeks, in which case the waiting period is up to 7 days. WSIB will provide coverage for disability sustained on the job and group insurance policy will cover disability off the job, with *own occupation* coverage up to 24 months and *any occupation* coverage up to 65 years of age of the insured.

Group Medical Insurance

This coverage is available for items not covered by OHIP e.g. a semi-private hospital room. If the employer contributes, he will get a tax deduction and benefits will be tax-free to the employee.

Group Life: the death benefit is always tax-free;

Group long-term care and disability: If the employer contributes, the benefit will be taxable on the employee, so the employee may wish to contribute through a payroll deduction. The waiting or probation period varies between companies.

It usually takes 31 days from the end of the probation period to join (i.e. submit forms and report for work) a group plan, otherwise the employee may be subject to a medical examination and other requirements

Group accident and sickness plans: see information on this subject provided previously.

Co-ordination of Benefits: The companies that offer benefits will liaise on group plans, EI, CPP, and WSIB; one cannot receive a disability benefit in excess of one's gross income lost from all sources. If a policy has a CPP offset, the government will pay the CPP benefit first and the group policy will pay the balance. If the insurance company compensates you and you also receive disability benefits from another source, you *must* return the latter to the insurance company *or the insurance company may sue the negligent party and give you a lump sum, after deducting amounts paid to you!* This is referred to as *a subrogation of rights.*

For example, single deductible $50, family deductible $150, and co-insurance 80%

Self: Claim for $1,000 – settlement for ($1,000 – 50)*80%

Next: Family Claim for $1,000 (1000-100)*80%

Tom	**Tanya**
50/150/80%	100/200/80%
No Co-ordn of Benefits	Co-ordn of Benefits

First claim must legally go to Tom because no co-ordination of benefits.

The company that has opted out of CHLIA becomes the first payer. If both plans have co-ordination of benefits, then the claim must first be presented to the company that employs the disabled person and then the claim may be submitted to the spouse's company, if necessary. If children are making a claim, then look at the parent whose birthday falls earlier in the year; if both spouses have the same date, then proceed alphabetically on the basis of first names. If the parents are divorced, then the claim will go to the custodial parent before going to the other parent.

In the case of joint custody, the claim first goes to the parent with whom the child is living at the time of disability. The claim goes to the custodial parent, then to her spouse, then to the biological father and then to his spouse.

25 Family Disability 80%	25 Disability 100%
Bob	Joan
No Co-ordn	Co-ordn
151*80% = 120.80	30.20

Insurance Industry Regulations

There are regulations that govern deposits to be placed by insurance companies based on the face value of insurance policies issued, re-instatement of insurance policies, contract information, unfair practices (e.g. churning: replacing with an inferior policy from the same company;

twisting: replacing with an inferior policy from a different company), licensing and continuing education.

Rebating

Referral fees should be a fixed dollar amount rather than a percentage, but you can split a percentage with another licensed agent. A replacement of an insurance policy needs a disclosure statement in four copies: one for the old insurance company, one for the new insurance company, one for the client and one for the agent. The old policy must *not* be cancelled until the new policy comes into force.

Errors and omissions coverage is mandatory for agents but does not cover fraud or criminal intent.

Holding out: an agent's image must be professional. Advertisements must be approved by the insurance company's legal department and one cannot present oneself as being a leading agent of the company.

There is usually an organization that offers policyholders some degree of assurance for their insurance coverage in the event that the insurer fails to meet its obligations.

Rating Agencies include S&P, AM BEST, and Moody's. These organizations rate firms on the basis of profits, reserves, claims, debts and operations.

Investments/Financial Instruments

Cash: Cash and short term borrowings, such as treasury bills issued by the government to financial institutions and corporations, provincial and municipal papers, banker's acceptances, commercial paper and bonds (issued by the govt. or corporations. at face value/premium/discount with specified interest rate, payment schedule and maturity date).

Stocks/Shares: Equity and Preferred shares are normally issued by corporations in an attempt to raise funds for the business enterprise.

Mutual Funds (MF) may be fixed income mutual funds: treasury bills, bonds, debentures or growth mutual funds: equity, debentures or balanced (i.e. a combination of both). Mutual funds represent a pool of money: a diversified investment managed by a professional portfolio manager i.e. active management (as opposed to indexed = impassive management, with lower management fees). The company from which you buy the mutual fund can sell the funds on your instructions, but this is regulated by the Securities Act and the Securities Commission. A mutual fund license is needed to sell, the sale is prospectus-based and the prospectus must be approved by the Securities Commission. The owners are unit holders and are protected by CIPF from losses due to bankruptcy of MF sellers, who are members of the IDA. Co-mingling is not permitted: MF companies must invest monies in a trust account, rather than misuse the funds in question.

Net Asset Value and ACB are always important.

Volatility, risk and rate of return determine the investments: money market funds have low risk/return, bond funds have medium risk/return, equity funds are more aggressive, mortgage funds invest in residential mortgages with CMHC insurance to cover o/s mortgages, where necessary, real estate funds invest in residential and commercial properties, specialty funds invest in particular sectors: technology, healthcare, transportation, etc.

Asset allocation is determined by whether you want fixed income, growth or balanced returns.

Segregated Funds or Individual Variable Insurance Contracts (IVIC) or Individual Variable Deferred Annuity or Individual Annuity Contracts are regulated by the Insurance Act. Insurance contracts are creditor-proof, tax free to beneficiary, and probate does not apply to them.

Segregated funds are mutual funds with insurance features: owner, insured, annuitant, the benefit does not go to probate on death, but there is no rescission period. One needs a life license to sell to holders of a SIN# (or someone who has had a SIN# at one point in time), who must be less than 80 years of age.

Advertisements regarding segregated funds must follow the guidelines of the Canadian Life and Health Insurance Association (CLHIA). If the fund is at least 10 years old, you must show the 1, 3, 5, and 10 year performance information. The owner of the fund contract is the insurance company that issues the segregated funds. The segregated fund contract stipulates a 10-year holding period, after which the contract matures. If there is one deposit to the segregated fund, then the maturity is 10 years from that date.

If there is a series of deposits, you must follow the terms of the contract, e.g., deposits as follows: 1st Jan 2005: $10,000; 1st March 2005: $5000 ... 1st October 2006: $6000 ... then maturity is on 31st December, 2016.

The guarantee is at least 75% of the deposit, but only if you cash out on the maturity date or on death, otherwise there is no guarantee, but only a valuation. Therefore, a segregated fund is an insurance holding.

Younger people will go for a 75%/75% guarantee re: maturity/death, middle-aged people will go for a 75%/100% guarantee, and older people will go for a 100%/100% guarantee. When a segregated fund matures in 10 years, you can change from 75/75 to 75/100 or 100/100 depending on suitability to age and other factors.

If the segregated fund is an RSP, the owner is the annuitant. Segregated funds that are not mutual funds are protected from creditors, *if the beneficiary is in the preferred class.*

The guarantee of at least 75% can be re-set to market value but maturity will be 10 years from that date. If you withdraw before 10 years, then the $\geq$ 75% guarantee will apply only to the segregated fund balance; penalties apply, unless the segregated fund contract allows such withdrawals.

There are two methods of calculating the revised $\geq$ 75% guarantee. The linear method is suited to funds with an interest base whereas the proportional method is suited to funds with an equity base. If one follows the linear method, the withdrawal is deducted from cost/reset value, but if one follows the proportional method, one looks at the withdrawal/market value x 100. This means that if the market value goes down, you should use the linear method, but if the market value goes up, you should adopt the proportional method, because you will receive more money.

Where the distributions/allocations are re-invested by the insurance company, you will receive a tax slip, and the tax paid increases will increase your ACB. Allocations are time-weighted, unlike those that relate to mutual funds. Capital losses are allocated to the investor, unlike in the case of mutual funds. Loads could be front-loads, back-loads, DSc or a combination. However, there can be no DSc after 7 years. Negotiation is possible only for front-end loads and you must know the calculation. There is no rescission and valuation is at net asset value.

Market value adjustment: the longer the period of the investment, the higher the return e.g., GIC percentage rate is higher for longer periods of investment.

Probate

On death, one's estate is frozen and managed by the appointed executor e.g. family member or trust company, who must pay the income taxes + half of capital gains (considered to be income, unless rolled over by naming the spouse as beneficiary) + probate tax/fees. The executor must obtain a clearance certificate from Canada Revenue Agency, then pay creditors and follow the terms of the will of the deceased person. If there is no will, the executor must follow provincial family law.

Annuity

An annuity is an insurance product that is creditor-proof and to which probate does not apply. This consists of a series of payments to the annuitant at regular intervals and is conceptually the reverse of a mortgage. In the case of a term or term-certain annuity, banks, financial institutions and insurance companies can sell, but single or multi-life annuities can only be sold by insurance companies e.g. RSP, RRIF, etc.

An *immediate*, as opposed to a deferred annuity, is one which makes its first payment within 12 months. The period before payment is the accumulation period and growth is taxed unless it is part of an RSP; a segregated fund is always treated as a deferred annuity. There is no suicide clause, because it is the investor's money that has been deposited and there is a beneficiary, unlike in the case of GICs.

Valuation date is the maturity date, with no rescission period.

Term annuity versus life annuity. In the case of a life annuity, if you die during the annuity term, the beneficiary will receive a lump sum or annuity.

Straight Life Annuity

This type of annuity is for people who expect to live a long time. If you die, there is no death benefit: (a) Joint Life Annuities e.g. Joint and Last Survivor and (b) Guaranteed Minimum Term Life Annuities: if guarantee is 5 years and you die in (for example) 3 years, the beneficiary will receive a 2-year annuity. The annuity may or may not be in an RSP or other registered savings plan.

A *non-registered* annuity can be a prescribed annuity: level payment including capital and interest, if Canada Revenue Agency conditions are met or an "accrued" annuity: a major portion of payment will be interest in the early years, and therefore taxable income. Registered annuities are fully taxable upon withdrawal.

An annuity can be indexed according to the Cost of Living (COLA), meaning that every year you will receive a different payment, depending on the change in the cost of living index.

An annuity can be a variable annuity, an impaired annuity (for people with health problems) or a structured settlement, e.g. if you have an accident, the insurance company pays you a monthly annuity.

Factors that affect annuity payments include the interest rate, term and frequency of payment, age, gender, single or joint account status and the guarantee factor.

Retirement

The government has certain programs in place:

(a) Canada Pension Plan (CPP) (if you apply) is a taxable benefit based on contributions (first $3,500

234

is CPP free) for at least 10 years. If you die, the benefit goes to your spouse and dependent children younger than 18 (or 25 if in full-time education). If you retire before the age of 65, the benefit will be reduced by ½% per month of age less than 65 years, and increased analogously for retirement after the age of 65.

(b) Old Age Security (OAS) (if you apply) is a taxable benefit if you are at least 65 years old and a resident of 10 years, but clawbacks apply for income over $62,144, and this benefit is not transferable to your spouse or children if you die.

(c) Guaranteed Income Supplement is tax free if you are receiving OAS and have a low income. *The allowance is tax free to spouses between the ages of 60 and 64, if you are receiving OAS and GIS.*

For RSPs the accumulation room or limit is 18% of the previous year's earned income plus the unused brought forward room minus the pension adjustment (PA)/contribution minus the past service PA; for an RSP account, the bank must know who the contributor, annuitant and beneficiary are.

	Own	**His Spousal RSP**
Contributor	Self	Self
Annuitant/Owner	Self	Spouse
Beneficiary	A	A

Contribution to a spousal RSP depends on how much room a person has. One ignores the spouse's income if the lower income spouse withdraws from the spousal RSP in the year of contribution or up to 2 years thereafter. The withdrawal is initially taxed on the higher income spouse, but after 2 years the withdrawal is taxed on the lower income spouse.

If you have a younger income spouse, you can keep contributing to her RSP even after you reach the age of 71. Canada Revenue Agency applies the LIFO method.

(a) Qualified investments do not include gems, precious stones, uncertified gold and silver bars, real estate, shares in a corporation where you have at least a 10% holding;

(b) Earned income includes salary, bonuses, commissions, royalty income, net rental income, alimony less professional and union dues;

(c) You can c/fwd RSP contributions to a future year, if you expect to be in a higher tax bracket;

(d) Maximum over-contribution without penalty is $2,000 as an excess balance, but you do not get a tax deduction for the excess payment and there is a penalty of 1% per month for excess contributions, *unless you obtain the necessary* Canada Revenue Agency *form, stamped by the* Canada Revenue Agency *and present it to the trustee of your RSP.*

If you withdraw from your RSP, you cannot get back the initial "RSP room" unless you take advantage of:

(i) the Home Buyer's Plan (HBP), whereby you can withdraw up to $20,000 as down payment if you and your spouse have not owned a home for the past 5 years. You can repay the HBP in 15 equal annual installments from Year 2 onwards: designate these as HBP payments on each occasion, otherwise they will be treated as taxable income; or

(ii) a Lifelong Learning Plan of up to $20,000 in total, over 4 years (with a $10,000 cap in any year) if you are attending a full-time course.

RSPs mature on 31 December of the year in which you turn 71, at which time you should convert to an annuity or RRIF and pay tax on amounts received, otherwise the RSP will be considered to be withdrawn and will be taxed as income on withdrawal/death unless one's spouse is named as the beneficiary, in which case the amount will be taxed on her withdrawal or death.

Registered Retirement Income Fund (RRIF)

Annual withdrawals in line with the minimum amounts laid down by Canada Revenue Agency tables are as follows: fair market value (FMV) of a RRIF on January 1 following retirement is $400K, and withdrawal is based on your/your spouse's age, but you must specify which one, for the life of the RRIF. The first minimum annual withdrawal = 1/ 90 years − 70 years = 5% of FMV; the second minimum annual withdrawal = 1/90 − 71 = 5.33% of FMV; the third annual minimum withdrawal = 1/90 − 72 = 5.67% of FMV, etc. After the age of 89 there will be 5 equal annual installments.

An RRIF can be closed at any time.

On death, the fair market value of the RRIF is considered to be taxable income unless it is transferred to the *beneficiary* spouse's **RSP/RRIF/annuity** or beneficiary child/grandchild <18 years old who will receive taxable equal installments up to age 18 or beneficiary handicapped child/stepchild/grandchild by way of an annuity or RSP for him or her.

Registered Plans

You can contribute from any age if you have earned income, e.g., modeling or acting role income or royalty income up to the end of year in which you turn 71; if withdrawn at 65 or 60 years old, there will be a deduction of 6% p.a. (as for CPP).

The contribution room considers RSP plus the pension deduction of the employee and employer:

1. Defined benefit plans. Employer and employee contribute to a professionally managed fund, to give you a

specific amount upon retirement. For example, it could be a 1.5% Defined Benefit Plan considering years of service; e.g. John has worked for 30 years and has a 1.5% DBP.

Career average plan: 1.5% of average income $50,000. Therefore, defined benefit is 1.5% x $50,000 x 30 years = $22,500 per year.

Best 5 years plan

Last 5 years plan

Fixed benefit plan: fixed percentage contribution for employee and variable contribution from employer, both of which are deductible.

2. Defined contribution plans. Fixed contributions by employer and employee. After the specified period, contributions become vested and can grow or be transferred to another plan or LIRA (locked-in retirement account until the rules of the plan allow withdrawals)/LIF/LRIF with spousal consent. The LIF

must be converted to a life annuity before 31 December of the year in which you turn 80.

If an employee leaves before the plan becomes vested i.e. within 2 years, then the amount in his or her plan will be transferred to company profits via a deferred (profit) sharing plan; if vested, he or she can leave the money with the same company or take it to his or her new employer or convert it to an LIRA, LIF or LRIF.

Government Benefits

The Canada Pension Plan provides pension, disability, survivor pension for spouse, allowance for orphaned children, and death benefit ($2,500 or 6 months pension). Contributions are mandatory if your annual earnings are $3,500-$42,100.

- contributions: 4.95% by the employee and 4.95% by the employer;

- maximum CPP is $850 per month from age 65 onwards; if you retire early, CPP is 6% less p.a. Therefore, if you retire at 60, you get $850 per month.

less 30% = approx. $600 per month. If you retire at 70 you get 6% more p.a.

- CPP is taxable; income splitting is allowed, as for RSP contributions

Old age security is a taxable federal benefit but you must be 65 years old and have been a resident for at least 10 years after the age of 18 years, with citizenship or landed immigrant status. The full OAS is approximately $500 per month if you have lived in Canada for at least 40 years.

If net annual taxable income is more than $63,511, OAS will be reduced by 15% for the amount exceeding $63,511, in accordance with the table specified by the Canadian government.

OAS with pensions of less than $14,256 will be given a guaranteed income supplement of approximately $7,200, with a higher allowance to a surviving spouse from the death of the other spouse, if he or she is between 60-64 years of age.

RESPs

Parents or grandparents can start contributing $2,000 p.a. (or up to $4,000 to catch up on a 1-year backlog) from the child's birth until 21 years of age. This is supplemented by a CESG grant of 20%, but the total contribution must be at least $42,000, and the maximum CESG is $7,200. The child can begin withdrawing from this as taxable income from the age of 18 years, for university or college education; the plan collapses 25 years after the initial contribution and if the child does not pursue education, the CESG grant will be clawed back and RESP of up to $50K can be transferred to your RSP or spousal RSP; the balance will be taxed as income, with a 20% penalty if the RESP is equal to or more than 10 years old.

Home Buyer's Plan (HBP)

If you are a new home buyer or have not owned a house for 5 years and you have money in an RSP for at least 90 days, you can withdraw up to $20,000 but must repay the loan within 17 years of the end of year in which you took the HBP. For example, if you took the HBP in 2007, begin paying 1/15 back from 2010 onwards, otherwise the 1/15 will be taxed as Y from 2010 onwards.

Taxation

Canada has a progressive system of taxation: the higher the income, the higher the tax payable, with brackets being adjusted for inflation; dividends are preferable to interest and capital gains are preferred to dividends and interest. Tax credits, such as for charitable donations, are normally better than tax deductions. Also

(a) Fair market value is important for deemed dispositions: death, related party transactions, switches and gifts;

(b) If the man/woman has a cottage, assume it is a second property, unless mentioned otherwise;

(c) Term 100 Joint Last to Die is best for estate planning to pay off taxes and transfer property tax free to family; only RSP without beneficiary rolls over to spouse and permanent residence transfers tax free to any family member. A 500K small business capital gain exemption p.a. applies on sale of one's own private corporation or farm shares in a public corporation

(d) Charitable giving: donation to a Canada Revenue Agency-approved charity gives you a tax credit on premiums, cash value and even death benefit of policy donated to charity. There are no probate fees on death benefit that goes into estate for transfer to charity, but one needs a receipt for donations to the Canada Revenue Agency-approved charity.

Estate Equalization

This is an attempt to ensure fair treatment of beneficiaries when liquidity is low because of executor's fees, probate fees and other factors. There should be adequate insurance coverage e.g., Term 100, to ensure liquidity in the estate.

Risk Management

You may reduce or avoid the risk, share/transfer the risk with (say) an insurance company, invest in a balanced fund, or take the risk.

Agency Law

An agent can bind a principal in various circumstances: an insurance agent has 2 principals: employer and client, whose needs he must address through

(a) disclosure and recommendations honestly and without duress, otherwise ≠ contract;

(b) ongoing administrative duties: delivering policy, making changes re: address, bank info, birth in the family, monitoring needs by keeping in touch; and

(c) conscientious attitude and maintaining client confidentiality.

Theft: it is advisable to accept checks rather than cash – do not use client's monies

Replace policies only if beneficial to the client.

Errors and Omissions coverage protects against torts that are not crimes e.g., fraud or forgery.

Business Continuation Insurance

This type of coverage helps a client to continue business in the event of death or disability of a shareholder/partner, etc. There must be a buy-sell agreement that states the basis of the valuation and buy-out of the disabled/deceased partner. The buy-out can be financed by an insurance policy.

(i) Cross-purchase agreement: a prospective buyer can buy a policy on a prospective seller of a business, or

(ii) Criss-cross purchase agreement: partners can buy policies on one another, or

(iii) share redemption agreement: the business buys policies on shareholders/partners and pays the disability/death benefit to the beneficiary/estate.

Disability buy-outs have a long waiting period of, for example, 2 years to ensure that the disability in question is permanent. Many companies buy life insurance and/or disability insurance on key employees.

Business Overhead Expense Insurance

This type of coverage helps to pay rent, salaries other than the owner's, utilities for, e.g., 2 years of disability and some other expenses, in order to help pay for business operations while the owner/manager is disabled.

T10 = Term Insurance for 10 years

T20 = Term Insurance for 20 years

R and C = Renewable and Convertible

NonCon = Non-convertible

Non-par = Non-participating permanent Policy

Par = participating permanent insurance policy

Joint 1st = Joint First to Die

Joint 2nd = Joint Second to Die

Bibliography

Ambrecht, John. *Estate Planning for the Family Business: The Non-Linear Approach.* Santa Barbara, CA: Ambrecht and Associates, 2001.

American Psychological Association. *Anger Class.* Washington, DC: Author, 2006. Retrieved from http://www.angerclassonline.com

Anderson, Eugene W. and Claes Fornell. A customer satisfaction research prospectus, in R. T. Rust and R. L. Oliver (eds), *Service Quality: New Directions in Theory and Practice* (241-268). Thousand Oaks, CA: Sage, 1994.

BBC News. Crowe 'deserved to be exposed'. June 20, 2002. Retrieved from http://news.bbc.co.uk/2/hi/entertainment/2055286.stm

BBC News. Crowe jokes about phone incident. November 28, 2005. Retrieved from http://news.bbc.co.uk/2/hi/ entertainment/4477178.stm

BDO Dunwoody. *Your Family Business Matters*. Toronto BDO, 2002.

Belding, Shaun. Dealing with the Customer from Hell. Toronto: Stoddart, 2000.

Bellenger, Danny N., Earle Steinberg, and Wilbur Stanton. The congruence of store image and self image: as it relates to store loyalty. *Journal of Retailing, 52* (Spring 1976), 17-32.

Berry, Leonard L. Relationship marketing, in L.L Berry, G. L. Shostack and G.D. Upah (eds. *Emerging Perspectives on Services Marketing* (25-28). Chicago, IL: American Marketing Association.

Blanchard, K., and Bowles, S. M. Raving Fans: *A Revolutionary Approach to Customer Service*. New York, NY: William Morrow and Company, 1993.

Blanchard, Ken. *Leadership Smarts*. New York: Honor Books, UK, 2004.

Blasingame, Jim. *The Color Of Ethics Is Gray – Part One*. April 15, 2003. Retrieved from http://www. smallbusinessadvocate.com/small-business-articles/the-color-of-ethics-is-gray-part-one-236

Blasingame, Jim. *The Color Of Ethics Is Gray – Part Two*. April 15, 2003. Retrieved from http://www. smallbusinessadvocate.com/small-business-articles/the-color-of-ethics-is-gray-part-one-236

Borden, Ladner. "It Begins with Service" (PowerPoint Presentation). Toronto: Gervais, 2008.

Bowen, D.E. & R. B. Chase. "Philosophy of Marketing," in *Service Management Effectiveness* (299-323), edited by

T. G. Cummings. San Francisco, CA: Jossey-Bass, 2008.

Bowen, John. Development of a taxonomy of services to gain strategic relationship marketing, in T. L. Childers, R. P. Bagozzi et al. (eds), *1989 AMA Winter Educators' Conference: Marketing Theory and Practice* (216-220). Chicago, IL: AMA, 1990.

Brown, D.R. and A.N. Angee. *The Living Franklin.* Oak Brook, IL: Oakbrook, 1975.

Carol, F. and Michael R. Solomon. Predictability and personalization in the service encounter. *Journal of Marketing, 51* (April 1987), 86-96.

CNN. Russell Crowe appears in court – Actor arrested on charges related to phone-throwing incident. June 6, 2005. Retrieved from http://www.cnn.com/2005/ SHOWBIZ/Movies /06/06/crowe.arrest/

Cronin, J. Joseph, Jr. and Steven A. Taylor, Measuring service quality: A re-examination and extension. *Journal of Marketing, 56* (July 1992), 55-68.

Crosby, Lawrence A., Kenneth Evans, and Deborah Cowles. Relationship quality in services selling: An interpersonal influence perspective. *Journal of Marketing, 54* (July 1990), 68-81.

Czepiel, John A. "Managing Relationships with Customers: A Differentiation Philosophy of Marketing," edited by D.E. Bowens, R.B. Chase and T.G. Cummings. 1990.

Czepiel, John A. and Robert Gilmore (1987), "Exploring the Concept of Loyalty in Services," in J.A. Czepiel, C.A. Congram and J. Shanahan (eds), *The Services Marketing Challenge: Integrating for Competitive Advantage* (91-94). Chicago, IL: AMA, 1987.

Day, George S. A two-dimensional concept of brand loyalty. *Journal of Advertising Research*, *9* (September 1971), 29-36.

DeCotiis, Allen R. and Paul Singer. The value of the ideal customer experience, ServiceSat.com. *Phoenix Marketing International*, Fall 2001.

Dick, Alan S. and Kunal Basu. Customer loyalty: Toward an integrated conceptual framework. *Journal of the Academy of Marketing Science*, *22* (Spring 1994), 99-113.

Drucker, Peter F. *The Daily Drucker*. New York: HarperCollins, 2004.

Dwyer, F. Robert, Paul H. Schurr, and Sejo Oh. Developing buyer-seller relationships. *Journal of Marketing*, *51* (April 1987), 11-27.

Edersheim, Elizabeth. *The Definitive Drucker*. New York McGraw Hill, 2007.

Fornell, Claes. A national customer satisfaction barometer: The Swedish experience. *Journal of Marketing, 56* (January 1992), 6-21.

Fredrickson, J.W. The comprehensiveness of strategic decision processes: Extension, observations, future directions. *Academy of Management Journal, 27*(3) (1984), 445-457.

Green, Patrick. *Family Wealth and Business Succession Planning.* New York: OSCPA, 2007.

Gremler, D. & S. Brown. Service Loyalty: Its Nature, Importance, and Implications. University of Idaho.

Hamm, B.A. Want a company you can be truly proud of? Try a business ethics program. *Compass Solutions*, 2003. Retrieved Aug. 17, 2007 from http://www.compassolutions.biz/id25.htm/

Handy, Charles. *Inside Organizations.* London: Penguin, 1990.

Jacoby, Jacob and Robert W. Chestnut. *Brand Loyalty: Measurement and Management*. New York, NY: John Wiley and Sons, 1978.

Jain, Arun K., Christian Pinson, and Naresh K. Malhotra, Customer loyalty as a construct in the marketing of banking services. *International Journal of Bank Marketing, 5* (3) (1987), 49-72.

Jarvis, Lance P. and James B. Wilcox. Repeat purchasing behavior and attitudinal brand loyalty: Additional evidence, in K. L. Bernhardt (ed.), *Marketing: 1776-1976 and Beyond* (151-152). Chicago, IL: American Marketing Association, 1976.

Johnson, Michael P. Social and cognitive features of the dissolution of commitment to relationships, in S. Duck (ed.), *Personal Relationships, Volume 4: Dissolving Personal Relationships* (51-73). New York, NY: Academic Press, 1982. 51-73.

King, Patricia. *Never Work for a Jerk!* New York: Dorset Press, 1987.

Klemperer, Paul. Markets with consumer switching costs. *The Quarterly Journal of Economics, 102* (May 1987), 375-394.

Kuratko, D.F. Strategic choices. *Journal of Small Business Management, 31*(2) (1993), 38-50.

Ball, Bruce, Garry Duncan and P. Leach. *Family Business*. Toronto: Thomson Carswell, 2003.

Lee, Barrett A. and Carol A. Zeiss. Behavioral commitment to the role of sport consumer: An exploratory analysis. *Sociology and Social Research, 64* (April 1980), 405-419.

Leland, K. and K. Bailey. Customer Service for Dummies. Foster City, John Wiley & Sons, New York 1995.

Lincoln, Yvonna S. and Egon G. Guba. *Naturalistic Inquiry*. Newbury Park, CA: Sage Publications, 1985.

Lyles, M.A., J.S. Baird, and J.B. Orris. *Formalized Planning in Small Business: Increasing Strategic Choices*. Oxford, Blackwell Publishing, 1994.

Lynch, A. *All in the Family Inc.* Toronto: Macmillan, 2001.

Marcus Z. Cox, Stephen F., Alicia B. Gresham and Stephen F. The Role of Customer Service in Small Business Strategic Planning. Pennsylvania State University, Pennsylvania, 1997.

McCormack, Mark. *Staying Street Smart in the Internet Age*. New York, NY: Viking Penguin, 2000.

McGee, J.E. When Wal-Mart comes to town: A look at how local merchants respond to the retailing giant's arrival. *Journal of Business and Entrepreneurship*, 8(1) (1996), 43-52.

McNamara, C. Complete Guide to Ethics Management: An Ethics Toolkit for Managers. Retrieved from http://www. managementhelp.org/ethics/ethxgde.html

McParland, Kelly. $200m is more than an "error." *National Post*, 22 September 2009. Retrieved from http://www.nationalpost.com/news/story.html?id=2017800

Miller, Danny and Isabelle Miller. *Managing for the Long Run: Lessons in Competitive Advantage from Great Family Businesses. New York*: Harvard Business School Press and McGraw Hill, 2005.

Monroe, Kent B. and Joseph P. Guiltinan. A path-analytic exploration of retail patronage influences. *Journal of Consumer Research, 2* (June 1975), 19-28.

Moorhead, G. and R.W. Griffin. *Organizational Behavior*, 4th ed. Boston, MA: Houghton-Mifflin, 1995.

Murray, Keith B. A test of services marketing theory: Consumer information acquisition activities. *Journal of Marketing, 55* (January 1991), 10-25.

Newman, Joseph W. and Richard A. Werbel. Multivariate analysis of brand loyalty for major household appliances. *Journal of Marketing Research*, *10* (November 1973), 404-409.

NTA Rand Council. Family Succession Planning. Can't Find: NTA, 2001.

Oliva, Terence A., Richard L. Oliver and Ian C. MacMillan. A catastrophe model for developing service satisfaction strategies. *Journal of Marketing*, *56* (July 1992), 83-95.

Oliver, Richard L. and Gerald Linda. Effect of satisfaction and its antecedents on consumer preference and intention, in K. B. Monroe (ed.), *Advances in Consumer Research*, Vol. 8 (88-93). Ann Arbor, MI: Association for Consumer Research, 1981.

Ostrowski, Peter L., Terrence O'Brien and Geoffrey Gordon. Service quality and customer loyalty in the commercial airline industry. *Journal of Travel Research*, *32* (Fall 1993), 16-24.

Parasuraman, A., Valarie A. Zeithaml, and Leonard L. Berry. A conceptual model of service quality and its implications for future research. *Journal of Marketing*, *49* (Fall 1985), 41-50.

Pritchard, Mark P. Development of the psychological commitment instrument (PCI) for measuring travel service loyalty. Doctoral dissertation, University of Oregon, 1991.

Pilkington, Ed. Bernard Madoff avoids jail. *The Guardian*, 12 January 2009. Retrieved from http://www.guardian.co. uk/business/2009/jan/13/madoff-bail-decision

Pinto, Maxwell. *Leadership: Flirting with Disaster!* North Carolina: RoseDog Books, 2005.

Pinto, Maxwell. *Management: Tidbits for the New Millennium*. New York: Xlibris, 2008.

Pinto, Maxwell. *The Management Syndrome: How to Deal with It!* Bloomington: Xlibris, 2009.

Porter, M. E. *Competitive Strategy for Analyzing Industries and Competitors*. New York, NY: The Free Press, 1980.

Prasad, Samantha. Tax and Family Business Succession Planning.Toronto: CCH, 2007.

Pringle, Gill. Russell Crowe: "Angry? Me? Never." *The Independent*, November 7, 2008. Retrieved from http:// www.independent.co.uk/arts-entertainment/films/ features/ russell-crowe-angry-me-never-997593.ht

Quinn, R. Moments of greatness: Entering the fundamental state of leadership. *Harvard Business Review* (July-August 2005), 75-83.

Reichheld, Fred. The one number you need to grow. *Harvard Business Review*, December 2003.

Reichheld, Frederick F. Loyalty-based management. *Harvard Business Review, 71* (March-April 1991), 64-73.

Reynolds, Fred D., William R. Darden, and Warren S. Martin. Developing an image of the store-loyal customer: A life-style analysis to probe a neglected market. *Journal of Retailing, 50* (Winter 1975), 73-84.

Satmetrix Systems, Inc. *Customer Experience Management Best Practices – Profitable Growth through Customer Centricity*. 2005. Retrieved from http://www.satmetrix. com/satmetrix/pdfs/sm-wp-CEM-best-practices.pdf

Savage, Jack. *The Everything Home Based Business Book.* Avon, MA: Adams Media Corporation, 2000.

Saxby, David. *Measure-X.* Retrieved from www.measure-x.com.

Scarratt, Malcolm. *Business Succession Planning for Financial Advisors*. Toronto: CCH, 2002.

Schwass, Joachim. *Wise Growth Strategies in Leading Family Businesses*. Basingstoke, Hampshire, United Kingdom: Palgrave Macmillan, 2005.

Sheth, Jagdish N. A factor analytic model of brand loyalty. *Journal of Marketing Research, 5* (November 1968), 395-404.

Silverman, Stephen M. Judge tosses out Crowe plotters' case. *People Magazine*, June 24, 2002. Retrieved from http://www.people.com/people/article/0,,624140,00. html

Silverman, Stephen M. Russell Crowe calls phone-toss overplayed. *People Magazine*, November 3, 2006. Retrieved from http://www.people.com/people/article /0,,1554602,00.html

Silverman, Stephen M. Russell Crowe mocks phone-throwing incident. *People Magazine*, November 28, 2005. Retrieved from http://www.people.com/ people/article /0,,1134863,00.html

Silverman, Stephen M. Russell Crowe sorry for 'shameful' conduct. *People Magazine*, June 9, 2005. Retrieved

from
http://www.people.com/people/article/0,,1070328,00

Snyder, Don R. Service loyalty and its measurement: A preliminary investigation, in M. Venkatesan, D. M. Schmalensee, and C. Marshall, eds. *Creativity in Service Marketing: What's New, What Works, What's Developing* (44-48). Chicago, IL: AMA, 1986.

The Superficial. Russell Crowe finally settles phone incident. Author, November 18, 2005. Retrieved from http://www.thesuperficial.com/archives/2005/11/18/russel_crowe_gets_sentenced.html

Trevino, L. and Nelson, K. *Corporate social responsibility and managerial ethics*. Hoboken, NJ: John Wiley and Sons, 2005.

Tucker, W.T. The development of brand loyalty. *Journal of Marketing Research*, 1 (August 1964), 32-35.

Ultimate Business Library. *The Best Business Books Ever.* Bloomsbury, Cambridge, MA: Perseus, 2003.

Wallington, Patricia. How did we ever get from George Washington's "I cannot tell a lie" to "I refuse to testify"? The Fifth Amendment. Total Leadership – Ethical Behavior Is Essential. Retrieved from http://www.cio. com/article/31779/Total_Leadership_Ethical_Behaviour_Is_ Essential?page=3

Walsh, Grant. *Family Business Succession.* Ottawa: KPMG Enterprise, 2008.

Ward, J. *Perpetuating the Family Business.* Basingstoke, Hampshire, United Kingdom: Palgrave Macmillan, 2004.

Wees, Aida Van. *Enhancing the Value of the Family Owned Business.* City: The Legal Outsourcing Network, 2008.

Weigl, Corina and Luanna McGowan. *Succession Planning Toolkit for Business Owners*. Toronto: The Canadian Institute of Chartered Accountants, 2006.

Wilton, David. Implementing Estate Freezes. Toronto: CCH, 2000.

Wright, P., M.J. Kroll and J. Parnell. *Strategic Management: Concepts and Cases*, 3rd Ed. Englewood Cliffs, NJ: Prentice Hall, 1996.

Zeithaml, Valarie A. How consumer evaluation processes differ between goods and services, in J. H. Donnelly and W. R. George (eds), *Marketing of Services* (186-190). Chicago, IL: American Marketing Association, 1981.

Zeithaml, Valarie A., Leonard L. Berry and A. Parasuraman. The behavioral consequences of service quality. *Journal of Marketing*, 60 (August 1996).

Patsuris, Penelope., Corporate Scandal Sheet, Forbes, New York, 2002.